Crawford W. Ha—

Y0-DRW-265

Sincerely

Mark Rich

RURAL
PROSPECT

BY MARK RICH

FRIENDSHIP PRESS · NEW YORK

THE REVEREND MARK RICH, Ph.D., Secretary of Town and Country Work of the American Baptist Home Mission Society, is a native of Oregon. He was graduated from Linfield College and Colgate-Rochester Divinity School, and received his master's and doctor's degrees from Cornell University, where he majored in sociology.

His pastorate has been entirely in the rural field. His work at the Groton Larger Parish in New York won national recognition. In 1935 he received, at the Northern Baptist Convention in Colorado Springs, the annual award of the American Baptist Home Mission Society for rural work.

Dr. Rich is author of *The Larger Parish* and compiler of *Rural Life Prayers*. He has contributed to the *Bulletin of the Christian Rural Fellowship*, *Christian Century Pulpit*, *The Baptist Leader*, *Missions*, and other publications. He has served as lecturer at the Union Theological Seminary, Garrett Biblical Institute, and at leadership schools of the College of Agriculture, Madison, Wisconsin, and the New Jersey College of Agriculture, New Brunswick.

He lives with his family in New Jersey.

COPYRIGHT, 1950, BY FRIENDSHIP PRESS, INC.
PRINTED IN THE UNITED STATES OF AMERICA

CONTENTS

To my wife

ADA GILLETT RICH

INTRODUCTION

IT is said that the church's field is the world. That is true, but the church's immediate field is its community, its local world bounded by the lines of geography, face-to-face contacts, interests, and mutual activities. No church can cultivate the seeds of the kingdom of God in the garden of the world unless it learns how to plant, cultivate, and harvest in the near-at-hand field, the community. It is not serving the community first and the world last, but serving both, recognizing that the same kind of ministry is applicable in the near as in the far field.

The community stands in relation to the church much as the first wave circles are to a stone thrown into the water. The enlarging circles reaching to the very shores of the lake are symbolic of the church reaching into all the world.

This book focuses on two principal topics. The first is the church in town and country, the second the community. For the purposes of the book there will be no need to redefine the meaning of the words "church" or "churches." On the other hand, since the term "community" as a specific entity embodies a much newer concept, considerable attention will be given to a description of its nature and characteristics.

The book is divided into eight chapters, which fall into three sections. Chapters One and Two serve as a backdrop on which is described the rural scene, and include a definition of the emerging new community. Chapters Three and Four consider ways in which the community challenges the church, and chapters Five to Eight explore the resources available to the churches in building the better community.

The author gratefully acknowledges the assistance and encouragement of many people in writing this book: those who read the manuscript and commented frankly, those who supplied information and materials, several typists, family and friends. Special thanks are due Dr. Mark A. Dawber and Miss Louisa R. Shotwell for preparing a statement about the former's experience, thinking, and action relative to church and community.

It has been a pleasure and a privilege to work with the committees and staff of the Missionary Education Movement.

M. R.

Harrington Park, New Jersey
January, 1950

CHAPTER I

Meet the People

Henry Jones had come back to his home town, after fifteen years' absence. During the interval, he had been engaged in work that had kept him abroad and out of touch with his childhood community. Standing on the station platform, he felt like a stranger in a strange land — a man not only without a country, but even without a town.

Then there was a shout, and he saw Jim — good old Jim Hendricks, running toward him along the platform. Instantly his world began to take on its familiar shape. He was at home again — he belonged.

Jim was a little heavier, a trifle older, but there was the same warm grin. His hair was tousled, the way it had always been when they had played ball together as boys. It was hard to realize that Jim was now the county agricultural agent.

Their hands gripped. "Welcome home, globe-trotter!"

"I'm glad to be back. It's the same old town."

Jim laughed. "That's what *you* think! Wait and see!"

Almost as soon as they started their drive home in Jim's station wagon, Henry began to understand what his friend meant. As they passed along the streets, he was impressed with the new appearance of what he remembered as a sleepy town.

Main Street had been widened to take care of increased traffic. The empty lot back of Griffiths' grocery, where he and Jim had

played ball with the gang, was now a paved parking lot. A new
town hall had been built and the huge fire apparatus could be
seen through its doors. A drive-in market had been built on the
edge of town, and instead of the old high school building there
was a magnificent new structure. Even old familiar places
seemed new in their spring garbs and neatly mown lawns. It
was hard for Henry to believe that this was the same town in
which he had grown up.

"Well! Things look pretty enterprising around here," he
said proudly.

"Yes," replied Jim. "There have been a lot of changes.
You'll notice it even more out through the country. You'll be
surprised at the things that are being done on our farms."

In the weeks that followed, Henry learned a great deal about
the transformation that had taken place in the community
during the fifteen years of his absence. He visited prosperous
farmers who, as boys, had been his schoolmates.

One of them reminded him, laughing, "Remember the time
you spent the night with me and we had to do our homework
by that smoky old kerosene lamp! None of that for *my* boys
and girls!"

Power lines, Henry learned, had been extended into the most
remote rural neighborhoods. The farmers were using electricity
in pumping water, lighting barns, hen houses, and shops, operating milking machines, coolers, refrigerators, deep-freeze
units, and hay dryers. They were welding, grinding, and cutting
ensilage with it. In the house, electricity was used for heating
water and a dozen other chores.

Farming practices had changed radically, too. The change
could be seen even in the pattern of the fields. Terracing had
lifted the faces of sloping fields, and there were numerous earth
dams. These supplied water for cattle, a place for fish, and
protection against flood and drought.

Henry found a satisfaction that was esthetic as well as practical in looking out at the deep curves of contour plowing on the hills. He was fascinated by the strip-cropped fields where plowing had left ragged fringes of stubble as a protection against wind and water erosion.

One day he accompanied Jim Hendricks on a series of routine farm visits, and Jim pointed out the way in which the fields were clothed in cover crops as protection against the ravages of wind and weather.

Jim remarked, "Some years ago an Ohio farmer wrote a book, *Plowman's Folly*, in which he opposed the moldboard plow. He created quite a stir of opposition, but some of his practices are being followed, nevertheless."

"Are there any horses left?" asked Henry.

Jim was quick to reply, "Hardly one. The tractor has forced them into retirement."

One of their calls took them to a hatchery where huge incubators, controlled for temperature, air flow, and humidity, mothered a half million eggs. Another stop was made at a farm where new equipment for filling silo had been installed. The machine was pulled down the rows of corn just as a corn picker would have been, except that it cut the green stalks, chopped them, and dropped the ensilage into a wagon. From there it was forced into the silo.

Henry said admiringly, "Looks as if all the backache is gone out of *that* job!"

Jim nodded. "Farming is easier these days — at any rate, it is a lot more exciting: hay-loaders, pick-up balers, hybrid corn, systematic planting and harvesting of our farm wood lots instead of the butchery we used to know. Agriculture is becoming more of a science — and a business as well."

"Are the changes we see in this community general?" asked Henry.

"Yes, they are. Say — how would you like to look at my scrapbook? You may be interested in some of the reports I have clipped."

Henry found a wealth of information in the agricultural agent's scrapbook, and read with growing absorption. Why, farming had become big business! It was being planned by experts and carried on by highly skilled specialists!

An item from the United Press caught his attention.[1] Agricultural officials had estimated that the chemical 2,4-D, a weed-killer, sprayed on Nebraska's fields, had added $4,500,000 to the state's income in 1948. There was a statement from Pennsylvania State College saying that in Pennsylvania alone 125,965 cows were bred by artificial insemination during 1947 as compared to 1,500 in 1943.[2] Another clipping told how the introduction of hybrid seed-corn had shot up yields to new records of production.

As Henry read, his excitement mounted. Once, when he was a kid, he had declared, "I want to be a farmer." Then, as he had grown older, he had seen — or thought he saw — that there was no future in farming. But now — why, the possibilities seemed unlimited! Farming was a business that needed an efficient operating unit to protect the large investments farmers made. The farmer needed experience in financing, making inventory, selling, producing in relationship to demand, world markets, and price levels, and in planning a long term for improvement of buildings, equipment, and land. This was a job to challenge the best in a man!

He thumbed through the book and came to a long clipping that caught his eye. Jim had told him about the "farm face-lift days" or "make-overs" in which conservation and extension services, farm machinery interests, and others combined their efforts to put on a spectacular demonstration of remaking a

[1] Footnotes throughout the book will be found at the ends of chapters.

farm. This article was about a make-over at Baxley, Georgia. It read:

Daybreak of November 3 found 1,800 men with 300 pieces of mechanized equipment moving in on the 1,300-acre Georgia Baptist Children's Home Farm, near Baxley, for a one-day "make-over." When the din had ceased and dust settled, these were some of the accomplishments:

Four hundred and thirty acres were prepared, limed, fertilized, and seeded to permanent pasture. Stumps were removed from 225 acres. Over seven miles of terraces were built. Three acres of sod waterways for terrace outlets were built. Four miles of firebreak were plowed.

Ten acres of woodland were thinned. Seventeen hundred tree seedlings were planted. Four-acre and twenty-five-acre lakes and a swimming pool for 150 children were excavated.

Three acres of grapes were planted. Twenty-four acres of fall garden were prepared and planted. An irrigation project for eighteen acres of vegetables was set up. Seven miles of fencing had been put up.

Technical supervision of the huge project was under direction of the Soil Conservation Service. They have been studying this farm for two years. Detailed plans for the big make-over were in the making for three months or more. Also cooperating were fifty-odd machinery, fertilizer, and equipment dealers. The Children's Home and Farm is supported by some 2,900 Baptist churches.

Materials used stagger the imagination. To mention a few:

Six hundred tons of lime were spread. Ninety tons of phosphate were applied and worked in. Over thirty thousand pounds of legume and grass seed and winter grain were seeded. Fifteen kegs of nails and five kegs of staples were driven. A carload each of gravel and sand, and five hundred sacks of cement went into roads, foundations, dams, etc. The manager of the Children's Home estimated that their property had been improved by at least $175,000.[3]

Henry, beginning to feel awed, continued to turn pages. He read about the startling developments in nonfarm rural enterprises. He learned that many rural industrial workers now operated with equipment and tools as modern as those used in any city. Some mines were being operated entirely by machinery. Processing plants, canneries, and servicing agencies required all known technical skills in maintenance, operation, and management. Rural teachers, doctors, nurses, recreational leaders, extension agents, and others were required to keep abreast of the latest methods and experience. The corner gasoline station and the village post office were competing with their city counterparts in attractiveness and utility.

Huge developments such as the Tennessee Valley Authority and those in the Columbia River Basin and the Missouri Valley were delivering power and light that had given to many rural dwellers conveniences and services never before dreamed possible. The familiarity with government programs, agencies, and services had put rural people into the mainstream of national life.

When Henry returned the scrapbook to the county agent's office, he told Jim enthusiastically, "Old man, I'm sold. If I were starting out all over again, I'd buy a little plot of land to dig in, and be a regular hayseed."

Jim laughed. "Not so fast! Farmers aren't called hayseeds any longer — at least, not seriously. There's a better feeling between country people and town people."

"How do you account for that?"

"Probably a lot of unifying factors have entered in. Here in our community, the new centralized school has helped a lot. It's carving out a new and larger community. It combines twelve districts. There are only four grade schools open in the country; the children from the other schools and all the high school students are brought in every day in those large buses you saw parked back of the school building."

"So we really have a new community — a larger one?"

"Yes, that's it, and the changed thinking and activities and opportunities that go with it are more important than any of the changed ways of doing things. A new community — I hadn't thought about it that way, but that is what it is."

Henry Jones and James Hendricks were concerned with changes that most people interpret as improvements. But not every change that has taken place in rural life is so pleasing as those talked about by these two men.

Destruction and deterioration are evident. Bad practices and neglect threaten the future security of the nation. America, like a profligate son, is wasting its inheritance in riotous living. Fairfield Osborn says that as regards the use of forest, grasslands, wildlife, and water resources the story of our nation is the most violent and the most destructive of any written in the long history of civilization.[4]

From 1909 to 1945 the nation's forest resources were diminished by 44 per cent.[5] One-third to one-half of the land originally used for clean-tilled field crops in the South has been abandoned. The enormous grazing areas of the West that Congress sought to control through the Taylor Grazing Act passed in 1934 are now severely overgrazed because influential cattle men have taken the teeth out of the law. Lumbering interests have their eyes upon the national forests. Only favorable rainfall has saved us from another Dust Bowl.

An airplane view of the telltale erosion streaks on once productive fields or the billowing clouds of a forest fire, a glance at the mud-laden swollen stream, an experience of a throat-clutching spring dust storm — these are but symbols of a vaster nation-devastating destruction that is overtaking us. The Soil Conservation Department reports, "For example, in a normal production year, erosion by wind and water removes twenty-one times as much plant food from the soil as is removed by the crops sold off the land."[6]

CARELESS LAND USE WASTES
OUR NATURAL WEALTH

WHAT SOIL CONSERVATION
CAN DO

It is not difficult to imagine the misery and degradation that follow in the train of this kind of destructiveness. It shows up in human erosion: in broken-down homes, in poor diets, in poor facilities of all kinds, in a decadent civilization.

Unless the trend is changed, America will go the way of many other civilizations that have collapsed. There is no longer a question about that. The nation can still about-face. But if we pursue a headlong course of destructiveness, the days of poverty are not far ahead for most, as they are now here for some in this country and throughout the world.

WHAT ARE RURAL CHARACTERISTICS?

The people both determine and are the creators, the beneficiaries, and the victims of the kind of society that exists. The end of all life is to achieve Christian personality. It is the people who count. Who are the people that make up rural society?

The term "rural" is an inclusive one embracing people living in towns of twenty-five hundred or less and in open country. Of course, some of these people are more urban than people living in larger towns. Likewise some city people are more rural-minded than their rural cousins. But for census purposes, the line of demarcation between urban and rural has been arbitrarily drawn at this figure.

The pattern of settlement shows up plainly from an airplane view of rural America. There are colored blocks of farm land with houses dotted along roads and highways. On the plains, houses are far apart and located irregularly at advantageous spots. In mountains, the isolated cabins and summer places are hidden in forests. In the hilly country, roads serpentine by pasture, cleared field, and forest, with few houses. Lake shores are thickly dotted with summer cottages and hotels. Villages lie in many patterns. There is a spill-over from the cities outward along highways. Housing developments in neat patterns are flanked by fields. Hotels and tourist cabins concentrate along highways. Then there are the fishing villages dotting the ocean shores, lumber camps, mining communities usually drab against the earth, dam settlements (increasing in number), army camps, ordinance depots, processing and industrial plants with adjacent housing. This is the way the rural population is distributed.

Some population changes have deeply affected rural society. The long-time trend cityward is shown in the illustration. The United States is going the same way as other heavily industrialized countries: toward gigantic metropolitan centers, scores of large cities, and hundreds of small cities.

The steady increase in the percentage of nonfarmers within the rural population is illustrated. By 1947 the nonfarm population exceeded the farm population. For the first time in our history a majority of the rural people made their living at something other than farming. So, the typical rural person is not a farmer. He may have grease on his hands or possess the delicate white hands of an office worker. The white collar is not peculiar to the city, and a man does not need to follow the plow or milk cows to rate as a countryman.

Another population trend is the movement toward decentralization. The American towns and cities are spilling over. Transportation arteries daily carry people out to housing developments, open country, rural residences, and small towns. The impression is that people, having exerted great energy in building cities, do not want to live in them. Factories moving out bring people with them. Decentralization is likely to speed up. Such bodies as the National Security Resources Board are advocating it as a defense measure. It is desirable from an "enjoyment of living" point of view.

The standard of living among farm people, gauged by income,

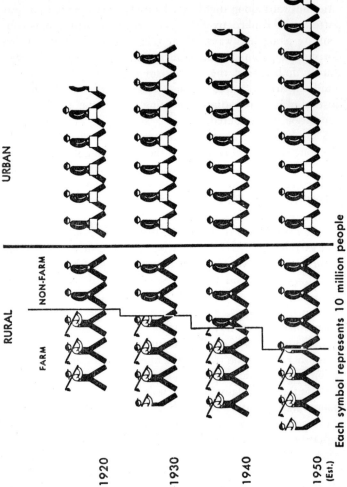

RURAL   URBAN

FARM   NON-FARM

1920

1930

1940

1950
(Est.)

Each symbol represents 10 million people

is much lower than it is for those not living on farms. See the accompanying illustration. This was true even during the period of phenomenal farm prosperity of the 1940's.

This condition is reflected in lower rural standards of living. Farm families have fewer conveniences such as telephones, running water, refrigeration, etc. than do urban families. A larger proportion of farm families live in houses that are over-crowded or that need repairs. In 1940 the average value of rural farmhouses was $1,419, and for urban homes it was $4,131. Fewer rural families than urban families have automobiles. However, farm families as a whole have better diets than do urban people, though they spend less for food.

There is a tendency to narrow the gap between living standards. Factors in the situation include better roads, improved school systems, rural electrification, emphasis upon parity income for farmers, the observation by rural people of high standards of living among city residents and "urban" people. If continued, this trend may eventually equalize rural and urban standards.

Rural people, economically, fall into three general classes. The upper third living in the safety zone enjoy incomes of $2,000 or more. Another third live in moderate poverty with incomes between $600 and $2,000. One-third endure withering poverty with incomes of $600 and less. This is a condition that fluctuates somewhat, but periods of high prices do not bring much alleviation to the lower third.[7]

A man owning three hundred acres of good land is a king in the countryside. His home is equipped with every convenience, including a stocked deep-freeze (or two) and refrigerator. He operates a new big car, and his twenty-year-old son drives a new model in the low-priced class. He pays cash for machinery and rests secure in a large bank balance. His income has expanded ahead of rising costs. He can take an annual vacation in

California or Florida and has saved enough in ten years to provide a comfortable retirement. He is living in a land flowing with milk and honey.

But to say that all rural people are "well fixed" is like saying that all city people ride in chauffeur-driven Cadillacs. In the same area with rich farmers, disaster, misfortune, and incom-

CASH INCOME PER CAPITA

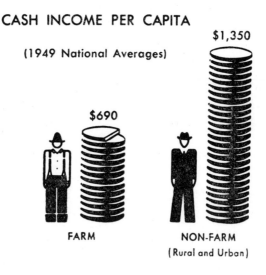

(1949 National Averages)

$1,350

$690

FARM

NON-FARM
(Rural and Urban)

petence keep many in a race between solvency and bankruptcy. Among the small town business men there are about as many struggling to keep in business as there are making a more than comfortable living. Many struggle along with too little land and insufficient capital.

Then there are the poor. There are many of them in the cut-over timber areas, the small towns, the hilly country, the farmed-out areas of the South and elsewhere. Their housing is poor and drab and their diets inadequate. They are under-privileged socially, intellectually, educationally, and spiritually. Included in this group are workers in the cotton fields who during the height of prosperity were earning $3.50 a day. There are also the share-croppers, each with a plow and a mule, borrowing against the next crop; the hired hands, the aged living on meager savings or pensions, and the unfortunate and discouraged. A sizeable segment of this group are migrants.

Country patterns of thought and behavior cannot be minimized in determining the standard of living. Some poor people eat well, dress well, have comfortable homes, and possess an air of well-being. Some people with larger incomes live in drab surroundings, are undernourished, dress poorly, and give every evidence of poverty. Given an ideal and incentive, many homes in mining towns, lumbering centers, and rural slums could be made more attractive; conveniences could be introduced and comforts enjoyed. The income is sufficient for a higher standard of living, but incentive is lacking. National, ethnic, cultural, and religious backgrounds are strong determinants of standards of living. Someone has said that one reason for the much higher standard of rural life in the United States than in Europe is that American women have insisted on having certain conveniences. The observation carries sufficient truth to give it a point.

Migrancy presents an increasingly critical, widespread, and difficult problem in American rural life. It has been made more prevalent because of the change of method in farming, by the exhaustion of soil resources, by the financial difficulty in getting young families "set up" in agriculture, by drought and dust storms, by the greed of those willing to take advantage of the disadvantaged, and by lack of resourcefulness on the part of the disinherited.

Reliable estimates indicate that 2,500,000 persons belong to the migrant group. Migrancy has long been thought of in connection with the harvesting of fruits, principally in California, and with the raising of sugar beets. Actually, it is prevalent even in those states thought to have more family-type farms and less commercial farms. For instance, in 1947, about 30,000 migrants found their way into the agricultural districts of New York State. Most of these were Negroes from Florida, Georgia, and Alabama. During and following the war tens of thousands of seasonal workers were imported from Mexico and the Caribbean Islands.

Migrancy belongs to all races and to most states. It is a national phenomenon, quite in contrast to the ideals of those early Americans who saw every man sitting under his own vine and fig tree.

Migrancy provokes many serious problems. Among these are the difficulty of a stable, wholesome family life, the difficulty of becoming integrated into community life, poor housing, insecurity and inadequate income due to crop failures, workless periods between crops, and inadequate health, recreational, cultural, educational, and other facilities.

What happens to a person when he is blown about the country like a tumbleweed by powers he cannot control? What happens to the Christian fellowship when people remain unsettled? What happens to democracy and to community life when a roving peasant class comes into being?

HOW ARE CITY AND COUNTRY RELATED?

Whatever happens in the country is of concern to the city, for country and city are closely interrelated. There are contrasts between the city and the country. From the writer's point of view, rural living is potentially much richer than city living. Yet, rural and urban do not stand in opposition. The two form the whole of national life. City people as well as country people need the abundant life. Whatever is the concern of one should be the concern of both.

An evidence of this mutuality of interest between rural and urban is found in President Truman's message on the State of the Union in January, 1949. He made reference to soil conservation, good land use, adequate storage facilities for farm crops, the extension of the TVA experience to other river systems, irrigation water for family farms, new housing, parity of income for farmers, and farm support prices. These rural interests, so-called, are really the interest of the nation. Likewise, so-called city interests concern all.

A new design of rural-urban relationships is being drawn. Country people are becoming more "cityfied" and many urban people more aware of the country. The style of dress on Ash Ridge and in Chicago was fashioned on the same designer's table. The accents vary more from region to region than from city to country. City and country people hear the same radio programs, read the same newspapers, and see the same motion pictures. Even in areas of tension the city and country are developing at least an awareness of each other. Conventions of rural people meet in the city. Many city people are keenly concerned about and familiar with the rural situation.

Former Governor Louden of Illinois has ably stated the dependence of the city upon the country:

The progress and security of a nation depend largely upon the kind of people who live in the country. The cities may be more splendid and brilliant. They are more likely to attract the attention of visitors from far lands. They may have a more conspicuous place in the histories which men write. He, however, who would measure the soundness of a nation and predict its future, will go out into the open country to learn what manner of men he will find there.

A city may burn to ashes and a more splendid one rise from its ruins; but when the soil from out of which the greatness of the city

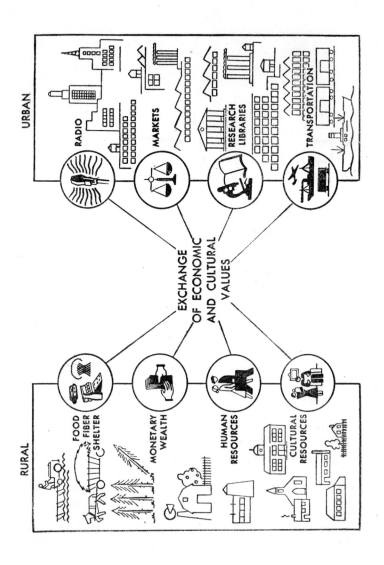

springs is once impoverished, or the people upon it reduced to penury
that city will vanish from the map of the world. History records a
long line of great, splendid metropolitan centers that enjoyed their
brief day — brief as history measures time — and then disappeared
forever because they neglected the countryside which nourished
them.

This may have come about by the exhaustion of the soil. It may
have been by the gradual impoverishment of those who till the soil.
It does not matter. For the maintenance of the soil and the well-being
of those who cultivate it are vital to any nation that will endure.

Those things that the country contributes to the city have
been summarized under four headings.

Food, fiber, and shelter: the things that feed, clothe, and
shelter the city inhabitants. A railway and truckers' strike, a
civil insurrection, or anything else that disrupts normal transportation gives vivid and dramatic evidence of this contribution
of country to city.

Monetary wealth: which gives power, comfort, and prestige
to certain city people. This wealth flows in for payment of
services rendered or products sold — oil wealth concentrated in
Tulsa, wheat wealth in Chicago, copper wealth in Butte, cattle
wealth in Wichita, and insurance wealth in Hartford and New
York.

Human resources: the people who move to the city, providing
for population increase. Leaders trained at the expense of rural
areas concentrate in the cities, bringing to it leadership resources
in addition to city-trained personnel.

Cultural resources: representing the interests, appreciations,
skills, achievements, and sense of values of the rural people.
The basic cultural values in American life still originate in the
multinationality communities of Wisconsin, the hills of Ken-
tucky, the plains of Kansas, rather than in the broadcasting
studios at Radio City or in the editorial offices of metropolitan

dailies. Unquestionably, the radio voices repeating in endless monotony the praises of some product of nominal value are also playing a part in the building of a national culture. Likewise, those in positions of outstanding urban leadership help mold public opinion, rural as well as urban.

Unequal costs borne by rural people need a word of explanation. The high percentage of children and of older people in the rural population makes supporting dependents a heavy load. The per family cost of educating children is high. Consider the parents who over a period of twelve years send four children to college. The investment would, if put into improvements, provide for painting the house and buildings, redecorating the house, installing a tile bath, a deep-freeze unit, and a score of new conveniences such as a washing machine, radio, television, and piano. Then when the youths have finished college they leave home. The investment is made for service somewhere else. This transfer of residence drains economic resources from the rural community. Furthermore, when parents die and estates are divided, the children living in the city get their share and thus pull to the city additional rural dollars. During the period of 1920 to 1930 it was estimated that these unequal costs transferred two billion dollars from the country to the city. A recognition of this fact may be one reason why some rural communities have a tradition against training young people above high school.

The city in our economy is important to town and country. First of all, it is a collecting center. It collects people for the organization and direction of business and wealth. Art galleries are found in the cities. One finds the rare book on rural life in a city used-book store or a great urban library. Even the old and rare stamp found in grandfather's attic collection eventually finds its way to the city stamp mart.

The city offers highly specialized services to all through

trained technicians. This is noticeably true in the fields of medicine, art, architecture, and scores of other areas.

In collecting resources the city always adds something to them. Collecting is more than a matter of filing and cataloguing and storing. The city specializes in styling and in making products both available and attractive.

The obvious counterpart of the statement that the country provides food for the city is that the city offers markets. The industrial economy that produces the cities has been a means of putting agriculture on a "production for cash basis." Gone are the days of homespun and production for home consumption only. In order for an industrial nation to endure it is necessary that there be a proper balance between industry and agriculture, between the city and the country.

The city offers opportunity for unusual forms of service. Many a country boy has gone to the city to become a national and world leader in a limited field. This is illustrated by the practice of a city dentist who serves a selected clientele — wealthy patrons from his own city, from other cities, and from abroad. When his brother back in the country dies a great crowd bringing banks of flowers gathers for the funeral. In contrast, when the city dentist dies a few friends gather to honor him, but metropolitan dailies and the professional magazines carry the notice of his passing.

The style of dress worn by young women in the sandhills of Arthur, Nebraska, may have the sweeping lines of the skirt Navajo women have worn for most of a century. But the Navajo in isolated Arizona had little power to popularize her costume. Only Paris or New York or some other style center can change dress styles for the nation and hemisphere.

Leadership in styling goes into other fields: customs, social habits, ideas. The city is making contributions of inestimable value through the dissemination of good literature, the radio ministry of eminent churchmen, the broadcasting of symphonies and operas, educational and benevolent services, and many other channels.

But, there is also the more sinister side to the influence of the city. Because the city is removed from grass roots living — from face-to-face contacts — it tends to depreciate basic values and tested virtues. For instance, the city-produced newspapers, magazines, television, and radio programs directly or through subtle overtones place a high value on liquor. Social graces are presented as more desirable than personal virtues. Likewise, these same agencies, directly or subtly, may give currency to both radical and reactionary ideas in national and international relationships. There may be just as large a percentage of rural as urban people who cling to these ideas, but the city can give them wider currency.

The city's ability to contribute to the total culture of the people becomes limited by its tendency to compartmentalize life, to shut itself off from the basic forces and facts of life. City people work away from their homes and there is more segregation of people according to interests. Sociability is enjoyed in the club or place of entertainment. There is also a strong tendency to shift personal, family, and group responsibility to agencies and government bureaus. In short, family and community life are reduced to a minimum in the city.

Basic culture arises in most vital form from those areas in which life is most nearly whole and natural. That is in the rural or near-rural situations.

Rural districts evidence a remarkable power to resist outside pressures and to maintain distinct cultures. Indeed, this is not always to the good. It is those parts of the United States that have been most isolated where culture has been reduced to its lowest state. The rural community needs normal and wholesome contacts with the larger world or it becomes ingrown and narrow. With modern means of communication rural and urban are becoming more alike. The city is making a tremendous impact upon rural life; yet the power to retain local tradition in the country is still strong.

The city offers the exotic, the spectacular, and the exciting. Great white ways, the brilliant theater illumination, the diffused lights of night places, stage shows, symphonies — these are part and parcel of the city. It is in terms of these that youth think so frequently.

For some, and some want it, the city offers anonymity to do what one likes without social disapproval and without being constantly under the eyes of neighbors. One can go about his business, good or evil, without all the neighbors, friends, relatives, and villagers following along.

Obviously, the state of the nation can be improved only through the cooperation of rural and urban forces. City life will be elevated by the best the country can offer. Rural life can be improved by the best from the city. The best from both will make for a civilization of higher quality than either can construct alone.

ARE RURAL PEOPLE CONCERNED WITH
WORLD AFFAIRS?

The American farmer produces for the world. So does the rural industrial worker who makes typewriters, textiles, and a thousand other products. The resources of the world are not balanced so that each nation can be self-sufficient. There must be an exchange of goods to meet deficits.

Food, particularly, is a world concern. A nation like England would soon starve with no imports. Single-crop areas need what others produce. The world population, increasing by millions annually, can only be fed with a world approach to the food situation.

World need compels interdependence. About two-thirds of the world's people live near the soil, yet about two-thirds of the people are regularly undernourished. The rural family, noted for their hospitality and sympathy for hungry people, in this day of rapid transport find it easier to have that sympathy widened to include people across the waters. The Heifers for Relief, Goats for Relief, the CROP and CARE programs, and others represent the outpouring from their barns and granaries to meet distant need.

Rural people have something to learn from other nations. In Denmark during the past century, the Folk School brought rural youth together for periods of study, and imparted a philosophy of rural life and a cultural interest that have made that country one of the best known examples of improved rural living. The cooperative movements developed in Denmark under the inspiration of the Folk School and in Nova Scotia under the guidance of St. Francis Xavier University have set examples of rural action and economic improvement that any nation can well emulate. Some people working in industry have established "productive homes," setting a pattern of living that stands in sharp contrast to the home that consumes without producing.

The prosperity, independence, and freedom of our countryside is unknown in most of the world, including our own possession, Puerto Rico. The whole world population if revived by a Christian concept of life would begin to climb the ladder away from poverty, ignorance, superstition, and darkness to a higher level of life. A Christian rural civilization offers so much to the individual and to the family that every rural person should want to see it built throughout the earth.

Rural people are becoming more clearly aware of their relationships and responsibilities in the world. Rural life in the United States cannot exist by itself alone. Farm leaders recognize the interdependence of rural peoples. National farm organizations in national session take cognizance of the world situation.

Rural people are peace loving; most of them have the hearts of builders and producers. They have much to fear from wars. War centralizes wealth and power and leaves less in the hands of the people. War devastates vast areas, blighting them like a burnt forest. The cycle of production is upset. Lands that should not be put to crops are plowed up, causing dust bowls, erosion losses, and declining fertility. Most of all, the farm and village family, the best fruitage of rural life, is interrupted and broken. The International Institute of Agriculture at Rome, Italy, established in 1904, recognized the fact that world prosperity will come only through world cooperation and peace. The rural people have a stake in world affairs.

HOW SHALL WE THINK OF TOWN AND COUNTRY?

The attitudes people take toward rural life are significant in considering the part that rural people and forces are playing in the nation and the world. Do people believe life in town and country can be good? Do they have faith that under God a new day can dawn?

There may be said to be five views of rural life: the religious, the sentimental, the realistic, the materialistic, and the practical. One writer expresses the religious view thus:

God lives on my farm, as, indeed, he lives on yours. His presence brings me joy and peace; he reassures me when my spirits sink from worry and despair. Should hail, should drought, should war and man-made strife overtake me, I turn in humble supplication to my God. . . .

In spring, his voice is vibrant and alive with songs of joyful birds returned from far-off regions. . . .

The suns of summer, too, are but a voice of God. . . .

His voice is that of lightning and of thunder. . . .

In fall, our God sends to us messages of beauty as all nature dons her gala robes to celebrate another harvest of good things. . . .

With winter comes a blanket pure of newly fallen snow. . . .

On farms, each night is silent; each is holy, too. Small wonder, then, that those of us who till the soil are deeply reverent unto God.[8]

The sentimentalist views rural life through rose-colored glasses. He may be a city or a rural dweller. He sees roses and daisies coming to full bloom without interference of bugs or cows' hoofs. Rural life is easy. There is nothing much to test a man, because the time of day in rural life is always a clear June morning.

The realistic view is taken by one who sees mostly the difficulties of rural life. He is aware of the absence of cultural opportunities, of mud roads, of disasters such as floods, storms, and drought, of poor housing and the uncertainty of markets and income. He misses the amenities of urban living and has nothing in common with the many humble people he sees in the country. He might be called a pessimist about rural life.

The materialistic view is held by the man who seeks first and last to make money. His back and life are bowed to that one end. He may think overly-much about money because he doesn't have enough of it, or he may be a man with a comfortable income who wants a bigger bank account. He plants more acres and builds bigger barns. All other interests become subservient to this one central aim. His view was expressed by a farmer whose home overlooked a beautiful river valley. When the extension agent greeted him, "My, this is a wonderful view!" the man replied, "But it doesn't pay the taxes."

The practical-idealist view is held by those who are aware of the hardships of rural life, and who know also how to overcome many of them and how to live abundantly. This view was held by the father who advised his boy not to go into farming unless he could capitalize on the sunsets.

One of the most frequently debated subjects is that of the advantages of rural living over urban living or vice versa.[9]

Where the standard of living, measured by income and physical equipment, is as high for rural people as for urban people, the addition of other tangible and intangible factors makes rural living a superior way. There are the satisfactions that come from having open spaces and from living close to nature, close-knit family and neighborhood life, and the opportunity for home production and flowers.

In spite of the technological improvements, population changes, and deterioration that have taken place in rural life, it should not be supposed that the basic nature of that life has changed. The arrangements, facilities, and conveniences have been altered, but the forces that give quality to rural life remain constant. As one has said, it does not make much difference in the quality of life whether one rides to town on a dirt road or on a cement highway, whether the floors are cleaned with a mop or with a vacuum cleaner, whether the cows are milked by hand or with a milking machine, whether the young people court in a buggy or in a jeep, or whether water is drawn from a spring or from a faucet. Life is still basically and essentially the same. The potentialities are the same; in fact they are greater than ever before.

References

1. November 15, 1948. Used by permission.
2. *Science for the Farmer*, Supplement Number 1 to Bulletin 502, the 61st Annual Report, the Pennsylvania State College School of Agriculture Experiment Station, October, 1948, p. 8. Used by permission.
3. "A Soil-stirring Spectacle," in the *Progressive Farmer*, Georgia-Alabama-Florida Edition, December, 1948, p. 15. Used by permission.
4. *Our Plundered Planet*, by Fairfield Osborn, p. 175. Boston, Little, Brown & Co., 1948. Used by permission.

5. *Ibid.*, p. 179. Used by permission.
6. The total annual cost to the United States as a result of uncontrolled erosion and water runoff is estimated at $3,844,000. This includes the value of the eroded soil material and the plant nutrients it contains, the direct loss sustained by farmers, the damage caused by floods and erosion to highways, railroads, waterways, and other facilities and resources. — *Ibid.*, p. 187. Used by permission.
7. *The American Farmer*, by Lee Fryer, pp. 18, 19. New York, Harper & Brothers, 1947. Used by permission.
8. *Successful Farming*, December, 1946, p. 21. Used by permission.
9. Recognizing that no list of advantages in rural living is undebatable, a committee of the American Country Life Association, meeting in 1947, listed the following:

   Rural life permits of more independence and freedom.

   There is greater stability of attitudes, thinking, and action among rural people.

   Rural people have greater security.

   Rural life is healthier.

   Rural people have a greater opportunity for property ownership.

   Better home and family life prevails in the country.

   Farm people have a greater interest in and a more constructive attitude toward their tools and other resources with which they work.

   Farming requires greater diversity of abilities, and farm work is less monotonous.

   Rural people are more religious.

   Rural living offers more community relations and neighborliness. — "Practical Ideals for Rural Living," by Joseph Ackerman, Christian Rural Fellowship Bulletin 134, p. 2. New York, Agricultural Missions, Inc. Used by permission.

CHAPTER 2

Rural Paradox

The rural church presents a problem. It presents an even greater opportunity. It is as alive with promise as are the chattering children who are so common in its congregations. It is as dull as the deacons nodding through a service. Its latent power to build sturdy Christian character and a self-reliant democratic society is beyond computing.

Some attitudes are alarming. Too many churches are interested in the status quo. Many young men have gone to the seminary and upon returning to their people have been found to have so-called dangerous ideas. The local church has been quick to brand them as modernist or radical, when they are only eager and in need of a little experience to balance their thinking.

Some churches are electric with eagerness and activity. They are the salt of community life. If they should be removed from the community, it would become so dull and meaningless that people would mourn as for the passing of a beloved member of the family. These churches are to the community what the coming of spring is to those who have endured a long and cold winter.

That is the paradox of the rural church. The prospect is so dim that it presents a puzzling problem. Again the prospect is so bright that it makes the blood tingle with anticipation.

THE RURAL CHURCH — AN ESTIMATE

The rural church had and continues to have an amazing influence in the lives of the people. Two rural sociologists report: "In terms of the number of units, of the total amount of current income and capital invested, of the number of people employed, population enlisted, and attendance secured, the rural church outranks all other types of rural social organizations combined, with the single exception of the public school. In some communities the church is an even greater institution than the school.[1]

Certainly the church stands with the home and the school as one of the three most influential institutions in rural life. Earlier the church ranked ahead of the school. Now there is a tendency for the school to outrank the church as the central institution.

The rural church in the United States comprises a significant part of the total church.[2] It may be conservatively estimated that one-third of the church membership and two-thirds of the churches in the United States are located in towns of 2,500 or less.[3]

It is a well known fact that as the country spring feeds into the city reservoir, so the country church is the source from which many city church members come.[4] The rural church contributes not only membership, but leadership as well. A New York City church administrator reported that of 86 missionaries in his denomination assigned to that urban area, only one had been born in New York City. That fact does not imply that the 85 were born in the country, but it does demonstrate the dependence of cities upon other areas for their leadership.

On the national staff of a home mission agency with headquarters in New York, of the 10 executives, 7 were born in towns of 2,500 population or less. Six spent at least 10 years in the country between the ages of 4 and 20. Only 2 were city reared and one of these spent 5 boyhood years in the country. These men carrying national responsibilities are predominantly rural in background and outlook.

It must, however, be recognized that in the future the city may provide an increasingly large part of the church leadership. This trend is evident in the student bodies of some of the theological seminaries. The appeal of the nondenominational shortcut Bible schools and the non-cooperative sects are forces drawing many rural youths away from the seminaries. Unless this trend is checked and the rural church revitalized quickly, its part in providing leadership will certainly diminish.

We have seen that the churches in town and country comprise a majority of the total number of churches and one-third of the membership in all the denominations. Yet, a large segment of these churches are outside the mainstream of the denominational life. They think they have little voice in making policies. They are not proportionately represented at national and regional conventions. Their leaders generally are not chosen to sit on national boards, committees, and commissions. Missionary speakers are not heard as regularly in the rural pulpits as in the city pulpits. A third of rural church people do not read church papers and are ignorant of the work of the church as a whole.

There are many reasons for this, and there is no one remedy. Certain denominations have recognized the situation and by various means are trying to bring the rural churches into the orbit of denominational life. Of course, many rural churches *are* conversant with the happenings in the denomination and feel themselves a vital part of it.

Most of the unreached millions of people in rural America are not far from some church. It is estimated that there are between 175,000 and 200,000 churches in town and country — one church for approximately every 280 persons.[5]

In American cities there are many more people for each
church than in the country, often from 2,000 to 5,000. This
difference is witnessed in the reluctance of urban church administrators to sanction new churches in areas that have less
than several thousand people.

The average church in town and country is small. The size of
the constituency determines this. Of the 750 Northern Baptist
churches in West Virginia, less than 100 can afford the full-time
services of a minister. Churches with 50 to 100 members are
common. In population-depleted areas there may be small
"shrine" churches that claim 5 to 10 members. Outpost churches
are often little larger.

But rural America claims some churches with larger memberships. The Steele Creek Presbyterian Church, Charlotte,
North Carolina, with 942 communicant members, purports to
be the largest country church in its denomination.[6] The Olive
Hill Baptist Church near Raleigh in the same state reports 590
members. The United Lutheran Church claims at least twelve
congregations with church memberships of more than 1,000
each. The largest is St. Michael's Lutheran Church in Tilden
Township, Pennsylvania, which has more than 1,200 confirmed
members. But the rural church generally is too small to carry
out its mission alone.

The rural church in America often is a competitive church.
Here are two Virginia towns with a population of 2,400 plus
another 1,200 living in the outlying areas. Fifteen churches
serve these people. In another town there are 5 churches for
600 people. There are still thousands who think a place is not
churched until a church of their own denomination is located
there.

Many of the younger ministers and laymen are deeply concerned about disastrous competition. One who has been a dynamic and vigorous leader in cooperation impatiently says

that the church is "fiddling while Rome burns." "The communities in this county," he points out, "as defined by centralized schools, have from two to ten churches, each one dividing the people into sectarian rivalries for the purpose of promoting its own existence."[7] Indeed, in some places the rural church is the most divisive of all rural organizations.

These are facts that cannot be overlooked by those concerned for the rural church. The terrible result is that competition when overdone weakens the churches and leaves many people neglected and unserved.

Some churches serve principally those of one cultural or racial background. One little town claims three churches of one denomination, one for whites, another for Indians, and a third for Negroes. These churches have little to do with one another.

There is a wide variation in kind and tradition of the churches in rural America. Most of the denominations are represented in small towns and open country. The extremes of religious expression in the United States run from the Hopi's snake dance to the high formality of the Roman Catholic Church. Even in the churches of the so-called standard denominations there is a wide variation.

The buildings range from little one-room boxes set on stilts to imposing, cathedral-like edifices with facilities for diversified programs. Stately hymns mark the services of some churches, while others take to gospel songs, choruses, and folk songs. Services of worship range from those with studied formality to the Pentecostal type on the one hand and the Quaker on the other. Some churches sing responses; others do not. Some choirs are vested and others would not hear of it. In large areas church cooperation is a part of the fabric of religious endeavor; in other places churches are isolationist.

Rural churches hold variant concepts of their ministry. Many are of the pietistic tradition, with a rather fervent theological interest; cultural, social, economic, and occupational matters are considered secular. Other churches enter into the life of the people through cooperation with many agencies and a broadly conceived program. A few think mostly of the life that is to come. Most desire a faith that is a present and future help. Some churches are alert; others are dull and lethargic.

After completing a study of church statistics, the Twentieth Century Fund prepared a pictorial interpretation of "The Typical Church." This was published in *U.S.A., Measure of a Nation: A Graphic Presentation of America's Needs and Resources* and is reproduced here by permission. The numbers on the chart relate to the following information:

1. Collections raise most of the $3,000 income; the average weekly contribution for members is twenty cents.
2. Church suppers supplement the church income.
3. The average number of members is 270; the church seats 240; less than half of the seats are occupied at Sunday morning services.
4. The minister's salary is $1,800; he has free use of the parsonage.
5. Car and travel expenses for home visits to members come out of the minister's pocket.
6. There are two sermons on Sunday.
7. The minister participates in civic organizations.
8. There is a Sunday school session.
9. The basement serves for meetings and special occasions.
10. The cost of maintenance is about $450 a year.
11. The organist receives about $150 a year.

This pictograph is included to provoke thinking. It is a statistical picture, not considered by the author to be a blueprint for a model church. How does it compare with your idea of a successful church?

THE TYPICAL CHURCH

TIME OF DAY IN THE RURAL CHURCH

The rural church in the United States has experienced three periods of development: the pioneer period, the period of decline, and the period of readjustment.

The pioneer period was marked by a rapid increase in the establishment of churches in new communities. Circuit riders, laymen, and settled pastors followed the westward flow of population. They led religious services in homes, in schoolhouses, and in groves, and at an early date saw to the erection of church edifices. Membership increased over a period of years. The churches were well attended. Being among the very few organizations, churches were the center of the social life as well as the spiritual life of the people. Ministers received little pay; pastorates were often short and the program limited.

But the church was a powerful force for good. It was established with the conviction that no society can be a good society without God, that Christ is the central integrating force in community as well as personal life.

There was a godless element in most communities. Some were rife with sin, but it was the church that kept the flame of faith burning in the frontier community. The church building remained the outward symbol of the pre-eminence of God in human life. The church made that faith real in terms of human fellowship and aspiration toward the divine.

One early American church was described as a very plain edifice. It never knew paint, nor plaster, nor cushioned pews, nor stoves to warm it. The people were warmed by the doctrines they heard . . . it was created for the worship of God and his honor.[8]

The period of church decline set in as the population began decreasing. This trend was evident by the middle of the nineteenth century. This was characteristic of many parts of the East. Toward the end of the century, observers began writing about the decline of the rural church. Locally the parishioners would remind their pastors: "We don't have big congregations as we used to. Why, this church was filled every Sunday."

The situation became so serious that thinking people were concerned. There was much talk about the "rural church problem" and about dying country churches. This was the problem-conscious period, with those concerned sounding an alarm over the distressing conditions. One of the earliest writers, observing the loss of population and general church decline, feared that unless some preventive measures could be found isolation, irreligion, ignorance, vice, and degradation would increase until rural America would be inhabited by a peasantry "illiterate and immoral, possessing the rights of citizenship, but utterly incapable of performing or comprehending its duties."[9]

Charles J. Galpin, in 1925, said before a meeting of rural church leaders, "Surely the Protestant Church in America is not well, when the rural flock among fifty millions of our people is broken up and broken down into so many unshepherded huddles and the wolf, too, biting at every flank — all because our Protestant secretaries will not pool their prayers and consolidate their power."[10] Dr. Galpin slipped into a common error of ascribing to denominational secretaries the miraculous power to repair the rural church. Otherwise he was an objective observer.

PERIOD OF READJUSTMENT

The period of readjustment took on momentum in the second decade of the present century. It has continued with accelerated interest. A new sense of the importance of the rural church is abroad. New ideas are emerging, one of the most compelling being that of the community as the church's field of service. The denominations are taking cognizance of the crisis at the rural crossroads. The awakening is local, state, national, and international. It affects the organization, program, outlook, and spirit of the whole church.

There is a sense of rebuilding, and a feeling that "new occasions teach new duties." It is like a spiritual spring-time when fresh, drying winds cause farmers to plant and think of new harvests.

The mission of the church is unchanged, but the critical nature of the situation makes its application imperative. This period does not hear the sound of hammers and saws as new buildings are erected. More characteristic is the mutual concern and travail of churches to find effective new means of service and organization. A new term has come into vogue — rural church movement.

The movement is not universal, but it is so prevalent that no one who studies the rural church can fail to be aware of it. The movement is realistic about the severity of the problems but hopeful about the ultimate outcome. There is still a critical rural church problem, but the urge to rebuild overshadows the concern about the "problem." It is certain that right now the rural church has a great mission. Enough people have caught the vision to give courage to many. To be associated with the rural church movement is a quickening experience.

These three periods of history are not clearly set apart, but they are interwoven throughout the whole period of church history. In many rural churches the periods can be marked. Others have always prospered; some have always languished. In most regions evidences of all three periods are observable simultaneously. This is particularly true on the Pacific Coast, where new churches are being organized in rapidly growing areas and in other districts at the same time older churches languish. In both old and new areas the warm breath of the rural church movement is blowing in new life, interest, and effectiveness.

WHAT IS THE COMMUNITY IDEA?

One of the most dynamic ideas that took form in the period of readjustment is the idea of the community. The trend is from a neighborhood to the larger community, from the small to the larger church unit. The neighborhood church's outreach, once determined by the "team haul," is now influenced and modified by the rapid transportation of the automobile age. Dr. Mark A. Dawber in 1937 observed and predicted, "There is now emerging a new community in rural society. It is the result of the new relationships that have developed between town, village, and open country groups. The depression, with its interchange of families and individuals of all age groups, has linked them together. This community is destined to play one of the most important roles in the coming social order."[11] The developments in rural society since then have verified the accuracy of this forecast.

A new community is emerging in rural America. This community is made possible by changes such as improved communication and transportation. It is affecting the total life of rural people. It is one of the most potent trends in rural society. Instead of declining in significance, it is arousing more interest today than at any time in our generation.

The interest in community is widespread. Sociologists, ministers, and lay people have been captured by the idea. Books and articles, conferences, courses and lectures on the subject are announced with almost commonplace regularity.

The word "community" stirs imaginations, for it is freighted with the idea of a new and better life. It promises changes and improvements. The phrase "the church and its community" has been so much used that it has a ring as familiar as "saved by grace" had in another generation.

Let us examine the meaning of the word "community." Dr. Dwight Sanderson describes an agricultural community as

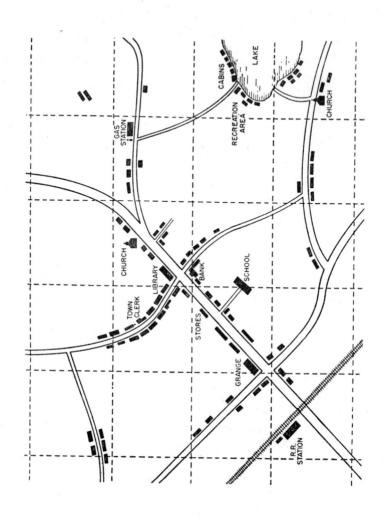

"the form of association maintained between the people and between their institutions, in a local area in which they live on dispersed farmsteads and in a village which forms the center of their common activity."[12] Dr. Sanderson's definition is the one selected as best describing *the community* as used in this book. A layman boiled it down still further. He expressed the idea that community is people and real estate plus cooperation or mutual love.

A first step in understanding the community is to draw a map. This is the way to visualize its outward form. First one draws horizontal and vertical lines as illustrated in the accompanying map of an imaginary community. The vertical and horizontal lines mark off areas of one square mile.

The symbols along each road represent houses and buildings. Centers of rural neighborhoods are indicated by churches. The large group of buildings shown at the central road intersection represent the village or town. Located here are the grade and high school, the library, several churches, stores, doctors' offices, the town clerk's office, the bank, gasoline stations, and other service and professional agencies. These agencies serve the village and the adjacent territory.

This community is made up of those in the village center, the two neighborhoods, and those living in the outlying homes. It is these people in their interrelatedness on farm and in village, on the periphery as well as at the center, who make up the community.

In determining the boundaries of a community one starts at the center and moves outward toward the edges to a line somewhat arbitrarily set at the points where the outreach of this and the adjacent communities meet. Rural sociologists have worked out ways of locating a community.

The community is complex. No one factor determines what it is.

It has a *geographic base*. One can walk or drive around it. It can be said that the community reaches so far north, south, east, and west. In many Eastern rural areas a community may embrace an area from twenty-five to seventy-five square miles. In the arid West one large county with a common center may be a community. The soil and all natural resources have a strong influence on the community. So does topography, including mountains, hills, rivers, swamps, and lakes. All physical characteristics, including climate, contribute to make the community what it is. It can be said of the community, "I love thy rocks and rills, thy woods and templed hills." Geography's relationship to the community may be compared to the skeleton's functions in the human body.

The community has a *material or economic foundation*. So, there are agricultural, lumbering, mining, fishing, resort and vacation, and suburban communities. The habits, customs, practices, outlook, and appearance of these communities vary greatly. The economic factor is one of the strongest forces in the community. Communities rise and decline in response to economic resources and conditions as a thermometer responds to temperature changes.

The community is *made up of persons*, each with his own talents, interests, and limitations, and expressing himself in his own way.

The community is made up of *persons in contact and association:* in homes, on the streets, on roads, in business, at play, and in worship.

The community is made up of *organizations* large and small, clubs and classes, coteries and sewing circles, auxiliaries, home bureau clubs and literary societies, lodges, legions, families, churches, and schools. It is a welter of associations and interests. There is conflict and cooperation, adjustment and accommodation. There is ill will and good will.

OTHER CHARACTERISTICS

The community has a *sense of oneness*. People share the same economic, social, cultural, and religious activities. At a higher level there is a deep sense of fellowship and of interdependence. At the best there is a sense of people under God living as a family. Then sympathy and understanding outrun harshness and misunderstanding. Cooperation outranks competition, and mutual aid rises above the law of tooth and claw. This feeling becomes so strong that people say "my community" or "our community."

The community has a *past*. That means that it has a *tradition*. This tradition carries from generation to generation, always with modification. It recites the names and deeds of the community's great. Local anecdotes, habits of doing things, mores and morals, the quality of school, church, and other institutions color this tradition.

The community has a *future*. This future, of course, is determined in part by the movement of population, by the continued presence of economic resources that provide security. Even more, this future is determined by what the people want the community to be, by the kind of dreams people dream, and by their ability to carry out high ideals.

The community has *balance or variety*. This balance exists between things and ideals, between free enterprise and government control, between competition and cooperation. The community is the social home where the person finds resources for full and complete living.

The community evokes an emotional reaction. Sometimes it is negative, as when a man says, "no good ever came out of this place." More often it is positive. A young lad returning home from college, upon catching the first glimpse of his home town nestled in the valley, experiences that feeling. In a wave of emotion the meaning of the community sweeps in upon him. The family, boyhood friends, the gentle hills, the woods, the stream, the church, the school, and other things associated with his childhood; memories of these stir him deeply. They all go to make up the place that for him has brought life. The quality of the emotion varies with persons and experiences. But there is no good community without this intangible factor.

The community has a *cultural quality*. The name New Glaris, Wisconsin, is known far and wide because of the Swiss traditions and customs it has nurtured. Some communities set standards of music on the folk level; others develop choirs and sing oratorios. Some specialize in dramatic societies and others in gambling. Louise Dickinson Rich, in *We Took to the Woods*, draws the cultural profile of many an isolated community:

No, poor Riches, we don't have plays and music and contact with sophisticated minds, and a round of social engagements. All we have are sun and wind and rain, and space in which to move and breathe. All we have are the forests, and the calm expanses of the lakes, and time to call our own. All we have are the hunting and fishing and the swimming, and each other.

We don't see pictures in famous galleries. But the other day, after a sleet storm that had coated the world with a sheath of ice, I saw a pine grosbeak in a little poplar tree. The setting sun slanted through a gap in the black wall of the forest, and held bird and tree in a celestial spot-light. Every twig turned to diamond-encrusted gold, and the red of the bird's breast glowed like a huge ruby as he fluffed his feathers in the wind. I could hardly believe it. I could only stand still and stare.

And then I repeated to myself again something that I once learned in the hope that it would safeguard me from ever becoming hardened to beauty and wonder. I found it long ago, when I had to study Emerson.

"If the stars should appear one night in a thousand years, how men would believe and adore; and preserve for many generations the remembrance of the City of God which has been shown!"[13]

The community has a *spiritual quality*. Some communities are established to glorify God, others to dig gold. Some are church-centered; others pay little attention to church. That there cannot be an elevated, enduring community without a deep spiritual quality is just as apparent as that there can be no personal growth without it.

Communities may be classified by size of population. For example, there is a small community in New York State consisting of a hamlet of 250 people and a surrounding population of 220. It has a central school, a Protestant united church, a Catholic church, a post office, three stores, a garage, a doctor, and a few custom work mills.

The medium-sized community may have a total population of from 1,500 to 3,000, the large community a total of from 3,000 to 6,000 people.

It is doubtful that there can be a genuine community with more than that number of people, for the neighborhoods will play a larger role, so there may be a division into two or more communities, or relationships of the people may deteriorate generally.

A Wisconsin committee preparing for postwar agriculture holds up an ideal of the community "large enough and strong enough to provide not only elementary but also secondary education as well as some adult education for all its people."[14] A community of this strength can also provide adequately for health, recreational, religious, and other services.

The words *neighborhood* and *community* frequently are used interchangeably. While there are instances when it is not easy to distinguish between the two, they are quite different. A neighborhood is made up of a group of families who share common face-to-face experiences. The neighborhood provides only a minimum of services. At the most there may be a store, a grade school, a community hall, and a church. Sometimes the neighborhood is made up of only a cluster of homes. Neighborhoods have not disappeared, as some have concluded. They play a central role in rural life. But the neighborhood is not the community. As has been seen, the community embraces neighborhoods sharing a common center.

Communities may be described by the way in which people are spaced in relationship to a center. First is the village center type. This community consists of a population center and surrounding population. Second is the open country community that is made up of a number of neighborhoods and adjacent houses. This kind of community can develop outside a city that is too large to form the center of a community. Third is the church- or churches-centered community. Usually it would be called a church neighborhood. It appears where the church or churches in the open country capture the spare time of people, direct their social, recreational, and other leisure-time activities, and provide the center about which most of the life of the people revolves.

ARE WE MOVING TOWARD THE
CHRISTIAN COMMUNITY?

How is it with people? Are they aware of the community in this sense? Do they envisage a community in which the spirit of Christ motivates the maximum number of persons and in which persons and groups work together to make the community a kingdom of God on earth?

Like the landsman moved by an identification with the land that he never expresses, people, perhaps more people than ever before, have a feeling for the community in their bones. A man needs his community. He cannot live without it. He is like the Cheyenne Indians in Howard Fast's *The Last Frontier*.[16] As they were fleeing from their prison in Oklahoma to their old home in the North, an interpreter reports their words: "They say they were dead a long time ago; they say a man is dead when his home is taken from him."

A man needs identification with the people in his locality — the grocer, the teacher, the doctor, the farmer, the ditch-digger. These men whom he sees daily are more than names. They are persons with hopes, fears, and loves, persons with families, with a past, with a future. So a man doesn't live to himself alone. He lives with the community. In the community he is bigger than he is when outside it. It gives him larger proportions.

Life becomes sterile, lonely, and futile to the individual who is not recognized in his own community. Such a man isn't a part of the people and the environment. He has no past, no future. He is only now. He has no dimensions beyond his own house. He is neither in the affectionate esteem nor the active disgrace of his locale. He doesn't belong locally. This isolation, detachment, and uprootedness is common in cities. It is too prevalent in rural areas, too. But where *the community* develops this is reduced to a minimum.

One may ask where the ideal community is found. Probably nowhere; the perfect community does not exist. But one could say the same of man. Although there is no perfect man, we do not give up the concept of man. The occasional person who nearly achieves full manhood confirms the validity of the concept and encourages many to follow after the ideal.

Communities, like men, are in process of becoming. They are always on the way. Many if not most of the people are not aware of the community. They put their first interest in their own enterprise, in the family, a club, a class, in business or the church. Some communities have a consciousness of common purposes and a sense of togetherness. Others are unorganized and disorganized. The community is like the train, not like the station. It is in process of arriving at an ideal state of human association, or in the case of retrogression, of moving away from it. Communities make advances and they also suffer setbacks.

One can no more do away with the idea of community than with the idea of the family. The chief problem is to understand what is involved in community and how to go about building or creating Christian communities.

References

1. *A Study of Rural Society*, by J. H. Kolb and Edmund de S. Brunner, third edition, p. 513. Boston, Houghton Mifflin Co., 1946. Used by permission.
2. The 1926 *Census of Religious Bodies* gives the latest reliable data. The 1936 census takers were not successful in receiving replies from a sufficient number of the clergy to give complete accuracy. No census was taken in 1946. Quite reliable estimates of the total situation can be made by adjusting the 1926 figures according to trends discovered in localities, regions, and states. There are also figures for certain denominations.
3. There is a variation in percentages from locality to locality. Of 222 churches in the Protestant Episcopal Diocese of Virginia approximately 160 are in towns of less than 1,000 or in open country. — From *A Study of Rural Conditions — The Diocese of Virginia*, by W. Francis Allison. Mimeographed, 1936.

   In 1926, 73 per cent of the churches in Iowa were classified as rural. By 1936 this percentage had dropped to 68 per cent of the total number of churches. — From *Some Iowa Rural Churches*, by H. Paul Douglass, p. 18. New York, Committee on Cooperative Field Research of the Home Missions Council of North America. Mimeographed, 1936. Used by permission.

   The 1936 *Census of Religious Bodies* shows the church membership in New York and New Jersey to be about 90 per cent urban. In states such as North and South Dakota the situation is almost reversed with about 75 per cent of the membership rural.
4. Shirley E. Greene reports the results of a study to determine the sources of membership in the Protestant churches of Terre Haute, Indiana, which has a population of 63,000. From among a carefully selected sample of members of 14 churches it was found that 50.2 per cent of them had been born in towns of 2,500 or less. This is a local confirmation of the generalization that the country church keeps the cradle roll for

the city church. The same study showed that the birth rate among these city people is falling below the fertility ratio of 370 children under five years of age to 1,000 women aged 15–44. This is an indication that for some time to come the city church will depend for its strength upon the church in town and country. — *Town and Country Church*, September, 1947, p. 1.

5. In 35 communities studied in Iowa in 1946 there was one church for every 405 people. In the same state in 1936 it was calculated that there was one rural church for every 470 people. — *Some Iowa Rural Churches*, by H. Paul Douglass, p. 18. New York, Committee on Cooperative Field Research of the Home Missions Council of North America, 1946. Used by permission.

   In many districts there are no more than 150 to 200 people for each church. In 27 agricultural townships in Pennsylvania, there is one church for every 259 people. — "The Mission of the Rural Church," by William G. Mather. New York, the American Baptist Home Mission Society, 1948. Used by permission.

6. *Town and Country Church*, September, 1948, p. 15.

7. James D. Wyker, in a mimeographed Newsletter, September 1, 1948.

8. *The Lisle Congregational Church — One Hundred Fiftieth Anniversary 1797–1947*. Lisle, New York, 1948.

9. *The New Era*, by Josiah Strong, p. 174. New York, The Baker and Taylor Co., 1893.

10. *The Rural Church*, by Charles J. Galpin. Christian Rural Fellowship Bulletin 37. New York, Agricultural Missions, Inc. Used by permission.

11. *Rebuilding Rural America*, by Mark A. Dawber, p. 135. New York, Friendship Press, 1937. Used by permission.

12. Reprinted by permission from *Rural Community Organization*, by Dwight Sanderson and Robert A. Polson, p. 50. John Wiley & Sons, Inc., 1939.

13. Philadelphia, J. B. Lippincott Co., 1942. Used by permission.

14. "Rural Communities of Wisconsin," Circular 353, p. 4. Ext. Service of the College of Agriculture, the University of Wisconsin, January, 1945.

15. New York, Duell, Sloan & Pearce, Inc., 1941. Used by permission.

CHAPTER 3

What Is the Church's
Home Mission?

If a community is to grow toward unity, the church can best aid the process. The reason is that through the church there is a grasp of the wholeness of life; it emphasizes the centrality of the spiritual to all of life. True religion always "breaks through" to an application to all of man's interests. It claims all of a man and all men.

The experience in the First Christian Church of Bethany, Missouri, illustrates how religion "breaks out" into community service. The men of the church became concerned that there might be more education for abundant living on the farms and in town.

These farmers, believing in the church and thinking it to have much broader concerns than just "preachin' on Sunday," formed a Men's Church and Civic Club in 1944. A summer farm tour was organized, with an annual caravan of business men and others visiting selected farms under the direction of specialists. The Harrison County Cattle Breeders' Association and the Aberdeen-Angus Breeders were organized and produced a marketing association that improved herds and increased incomes to the farmers.

Through the club, a limestone quarry was discovered and developed. A Limestone Field Day drew an attendance of

2,000, and a tractor-plowing contest in 1947 brought together 5,000. These celebrations were encouraged in the interest of conserving and building up the soil.

The father of the club idea, W. M. Planck, says that the men deliberately set out to make this a phase of the church program. "There is a need for the church to attract and make the men like something. The people need the interest of the church for progress, to make the community more provident, and to make all good things better. That's why the men's club was formed."[1]

Apparently Bethany people like a church that includes in its interest this kind of activity, for it is reported that each Sunday morning both townspeople and farmers stream through the doors of the church to worship God. Roots in the soil make a strong church.

Besides having a large place in the life of the person and of the family, the church has another role; that is to create the community. The church's ideals are to be incarnated in personal and family life, but also in industrial effort and political development and in all social relationships. The community role is even more imperative today when rural life is shifting and changing.

The church is a specialist in life. In it are the potentials to envision the highest form of life for the person and for society. No other institution has the resources of the church out of which to create the vision of a blessed community. Do we not have as Master the one who said, "I came that they may have life and may have it abundantly"? It is no stretch of the imagination to apply this promise to the people living contiguously in an area, the community.

The Christian ideal of the community envisages an area in which the people move individually and corporately by the power of Christ, blossom and bear fruitage in character, service, enterprise, and fellowship. It is a place where people so live that all the elements with which God has endowed the community combine to make the people good children of God and their relationships characteristic of the family of God. Just as a choir made up of many ordinary voices and a few soloists makes heavenly harmony, so people may live together in an area to become greater than any one person or group. The community can become far greater than the sum total of the people.

The church is interested in its own strength only as it serves to build Christ into the character of the people and their relationships and institutions. Here is an expression of it:

I believe in the Rural Church. I believe its progress is fundamental to the future welfare of our Nation.

I believe in the Rural Community; in its neighborliness; in its serving institutions; in its creative environment of understanding and sympathy.

I believe in Rural People; in the integrity of the men and women of the soil; in the hopes and dreams of their sons and daughters; in their need for the Christ.

I believe in the Rural Christ. He was one who loved the flocks and the fields, the birds and the trees, ripening wheat bending before the clean-blowing breeze. He loved the sons of the soil.

I believe a new day dawns for Christianizing Rural Life, the children of the countryside, Rural Communities and their institutions. I covet Rural Life for Christ. I believe Community Religion is essential to a present day portrayal of Christ. I rejoice to have some part in the growth toward a Christian America.

I believe in the Rural Church.[2]

The church can contribute the one ingredient most important to community development — the Christian faith. The church's duty, but even more its privilege, is to keep the power and beauty and love of Christ the central, moving force in the community. Only so can there be good communities.

When the idea of community impresses itself upon the church, immediately changes begin to occur. These changes affect the conception of a church's task in the community, intensify some concerns, enlarge the service, and cause the church to seek to meet the basic needs of people. They lead churches to make membership adjustment, to reorganize, and to cooperate with other churches and with constructive community forces. When the community idea imbues the life of churches, the changes that occur are as far-reaching as those wrought by the Reformation.

HOW DOES THE COMMUNITY IDEAL
AFFECT THE CHURCH?

One of the first practical results of a vision of the community is the church's awakening concern *for all the people in the community*. Not only the people at the center, but those at the periphery need to be served. The rich, the poor, the newcomer, the old-timer, the business man, the factory worker, the young, the old, the hardened reprobate, and the saint; those all are the concern of the church. Because they live in the area of the community God's love constrains the church to include them. As a Texas rural churchman put it, "We should go out beyond the church into the homes — into the community. That's the only way we can help people."

This desire to serve attempts to correct the evil of fragmentation and overlooking people. The church has sinned greatly against its own ideal. Fragmentation and division of the community have been too much a part and parcel of church effort.

The rural church is too much a class church economically, socially, and culturally. In some communities each church tends to serve a different class. The "standard" denomination has become very much a middle class church. The church's practice has been to "multiply by division" instead of increasing by union. This tendency to serve a segment of the community results in neglecting people. Among those unreached and overlooked are groups that present a particular concern to the community-serving church.

First are the "roving, rambling people" who move from field to field and from crop to crop. These 2½ million are rootless, footloose, without security, without community, and often without church. Despite notable exceptions, the local churches have overlooked these in their ministry, or, being concerned, have not known what to do.

Second are the tenants, hired hands, and others whose residence and rootage in the community are longer than that of migrants but not permanent.

Third is the outer circle of the community. Some of the early rural church surveys made thirty-five years ago revealed a condition that has persisted to the present. It can be illustrated by drawing a map. At distances representing a mile apart, draw concentric circles with the church at the center. A study of church attendance and participation showed that each succeeding circular area outward included a smaller percentage of persons participating in the life of the church. It is a frequently noted fact that the outer reaches of the church's influence, often the edge of the community, have been poorly served and only a minority of the people reached.[3]

It has been rather complacently taken for granted that the American farmer is a church-going person. A study in Pennsylvania shakes any such smug complacency. This study made in 27 sample rural agricultural townships shows only 44.5 per cent of the population on the church rolls as compared to 53 per cent for the United States as a whole.[4] Since the farmer is among the unreached groups, that should give the church more concern than it has evidenced of late.

One reason that so many people have been neglected by the

church is that the system of caring for them is inadequate. The church proclaims that its great, eternal mission is to embrace all. It says that God is no respector of persons and that all men are of one blood. But the basic ideas motivating church membership — fellowship and organization — have been so institutionalized as to separate people from one another and to result in the neglect of people.

The story of the Reverend J. E. Wright is a heartening example of a ministry that provided the intensive and effective pastoral outreach envisioned by most Christian churches. During the years 1920 to 1944, Mr. Wright was minister of a large rural Negro parish in Middlesex County, Virginia. Coming from the lumbering business into the pastorate, he led his church in an amazing program of service and outreach. His engaging personality and his leadership ability made him a great man in his community. A record of his ministry appears in *One Foot on the Land*, by Ralph A. Felton.[5]

Mr. Wright's observation over a period of years as a resident in this one rural parish led him to the conclusion that people "go to the devil" between Sundays. Serving the people as their minister, he thought, was much more than preaching gospel sermons on Sundays. He used to say, "We go into the church to worship; we go out of the church to serve." It's what this pastor did the six days of the week during his twenty-four years' ministry that gave him the most satisfaction.

Mr. Wright was personally responsible for building a centralized school. He taught the people to cooperate in the purchase of fertilizer, he introduced the extensive cultivation of cucumbers, thus helping the people increase their cash incomes, and he demonstrated successful methods of raising wheat. He encouraged baseball and other forms of recreation. His advocacy of home ownership increased largely the number of home owners; he urged the extension of electric lines and home improvement; he advised people to have bank accounts and to pay bills by check. He operated a school bus, he taught school, he organized yearly trips to historic places, he organized clubs, and he bought a poultry farm and experimented with egg production, thus introducing a profitable system of poultry raising.

Mr. Wright did all this and more while he was pastor of two churches. All the while he stated firmly that he was first and foremost a minister of the gospel. The results of his work are amazing. During his ministry of twenty-four years in this one parish it became a church-centered community. It was claimed that as a result only four Negroes over ten years of age in the southern half of the county were not church members.

Another practical result of the community ideal is new hope in the idea of parish. Sometimes this is called the "geographic approach." Like many other ideas and concepts, it is both old and sound. It is also compatible with the genius of Protestantism. The parish approach may be described as the concern of the church or churches to serve every person in a geographic area, and a realistic technique for carrying out this concern. To introduce this plan would revolutionize Protestantism. It would not in itself solve problems, but it is a good process through which the purposes of God and Christ could be carried out more fully in the community.

The parish plan stimulates evangelism by offering a new framework and impetus for it.

The purpose of the church is to win people to God through Christ. The lost sheep, the lost coin, the lost son are examples of lostness. A man can be lost like that. The church's concern is that the sheep be in one fold, that none be overlooked, that none be sequestered on a mountain crag, left out to exposure and danger. The idea of community and parish challenges at this point.

There are lost people in the rural districts: those in whom

no candles of the spirit have been lighted, those unconcerned for self, for others, and the community, those whose work is their God, those who live to build bigger barns and to extend the boundaries of their farms, those who live well by keeping others poor, and those whose vision is shut in as with blinders.

Then there are those whose spirits are not right, the self-centered, the uncharitable, the harshly critical, the bitter and resentful, those whose hearts are closed to the influences of the spirit. The careless, the profligate, and the drunkard are in every community, and those whose lives have yielded to the passions of lust. Children grow up in homes where the doors are closed against Christ; communities are held back by those chronically opposed to change and to any step that costs money, labor, or effort.

Bigotry, narrow-mindedness, and exclusiveness are common. Some are only shy and timid or are thwarted by feelings of inferiority. Others are outcasts in their own minds. All are in need of being much bigger and more able and far-seeing.

Here, then, are the people to be reached. The ideas of community and parish can provide a bridge between them and the church.

Some churches, most evangelistic in word and least evangelistic in fact, have not gotten down to brass tacks as to who and where the unreached are. The church with a parish concept is on the road to a larger plan of evangelism because of the concern for all the people. As has been noted, a lone church in a community has all the people in the area in its field. Where there is more than one church, all the people still are the concern of the churches. There is as much concern for the family in the last house on the last road or the family in the isolated "holler" as for the families under the eaves of the church.

It may be said that this concept of evangelism makes churches population-minded as well as person-minded. Because a person is living in the community, he is the responsibility of the church.

John Frederic Oberlin [6] kept a list of every person in his parish, with important facts about each. He wanted to know "the sheep and the lambs" of his flock, *all* the sheep and *all* the lambs, so he might better bring them into Christian fellowship. Richard Baxter, the eminent seventeenth century English pastor, preached as "a dying man to dying men." The depth of his concern is evident in his pastoral ministry, which was inclusive of every family and each member of every family in the whole parish. He made an arrangement whereby each of his eight hundred families could once a year spend an hour in conference with him.

See the challenge of his idea of evangelism — to state, national, and world evangelism! Start with a single county. Divide it into communities, leaving no spaces unassigned, no neglected corridors. Then let the churches in each community work to provide a ministry to all people in the area. Extend the plan to adjacent counties, to the state, to the nation, to the world. Of course, some potential community areas need to be determined somewhat arbitrarily, for some people will choose to affiliate with churches outside their community and some will withstand the ministry of any church. Nevertheless, with such an approach diligently followed, the churches will include more people than ever before.

This approach is needed in the great rural nations of the world, in Latin America, India, China, and Africa. In modified form it applies to the city that cannot be reached as a whole but only as divided into "manageable" communities. America and the rest of the world are crying for such a program.

There can be no satisfactory method of evangelism without the community ideal and the parish plan. There can be no sufficient service and outreach, and eventually no full-fledged church without it.

WHAT IS REQUIRED FOR
EFFECTIVE COMMUNITY SERVICE?

When a church becomes imbued with the community idea, some interests, insights, and concerns are intensified. The church that becomes aware of *the community* has a new insight into the needs of the community. The church's eyes are made clear-sighted, so it observes certain needs not before recognized as needs and others that before were of no concern to it. These needs are (1) apparent, obvious, or outward needs, and (2) deep-seated and outwardly less obvious needs that might be described as deficiencies in the community's spirit.

Not long ago on a trip through a certain state, a traveler was struck with several apparent needs obvious to anyone who had eyes to see and ears to hear. From train, bus, and automobile his eyes fell on unpleasant sights in small towns.

Yards were littered with old lumber, weeds, branches, tin cans, rubbish, and miscellaneous debris. This was especially true along the railways and in the outskirts of villages. Many towns presented a dismal aspect. There was much poor housing: shacks with weatherbeaten boards patched with tin. The wind could drive in, the dust drift in, and the mud track in. Many people had little more than a squatter existence in homes with interiors and exteriors equally drab and desolate.

Many fields were exposed to erosion, with water cutting gullies in octopus-like patterns. Wind was driving clouds of dust from the peanut fields, though it was still the wet season. A charge was being made against future generations, one that if not checked would run a bill so big it could never be paid.

In a drug store a lone copy of the *New Republic* was flanked by *Pin-up Girl* and even less desirable publications. Magazine racks throughout this area commonly displayed rows of trash, some only shallow, some suggestive and lewd. The billboards advertising motion pictures indicated trite, cheap, and frothy showings. There seemed to be few adequate recreational facilities.

In a bus station a minister pointed out three handsome young men. "Those men represent the type of person we are not reaching," he said. "These boys were in the Army. They have ability, but they are not preparing themselves for any position of responsibility; they live from hand to mouth; they are not building up their homes. The church has been unable to reach them." Those three are a symbol of the thousands of unreached youths in country places without Christian motivation.

The color line was evident in many towns. These towns had four washrooms in the stations, two each for Negroes and whites. Restaurants, too, had their "standards," and there was considerable segregation in housing.

These are obvious needs. Perhaps some of them are only surface needs that if remedied would only improve the outward appearance but not touch the heart of the community. Others indicate deeply lodged ailments not easily cured.

The church, challenged by the idea of the community, will also see the deeper needs. Many communities are torn by tensions, antagonisms, feuds, divisions, and class feeling that destroy and prevent unity and harmony. Lives are blighted by habits and attitudes born out of personal selfishness, greed, and carelessness, and often by conditions in the community. There are people who block the path of good will and progress. Others are so provincial and so bound by tradition that they never receive a new idea from outside or leave the past for the present or future.

The church looking at the community will see sin in individual and corporate form. The community as a whole as well as the individuals in it need redemption from folly, from blindness, wickedness, and sin.

To see the community as a strong educational force is a challenge that the concept of *the community* brings to the church. The educational forces in a community are usually quickly listed as the school, the family, Sunday school classes, and certain clubs and societies. These are the agencies set up to educate and train the people.

But, actually, *the community as a whole* is the strongest educational force. The generally accepted moral codes and mores of the citizenry have a tremendously strong teaching power. The outlook and practices of factory workers, merchants, and professional men, and what happens in the gang, are all powerful influences in the lives of developing youth. The unexpressed goals for living, everything a community is and does, is a vital influence in building or destroying character. The community is to persons what the garden is to plants.

The community can easily be at odds with the church and other constructive agencies in its teachings. In Sunday school a boy learns "Thou shalt not steal"; the gang may teach him that it is smart to steal. The 4-H Club imparts information about and encourages practices of soil conservation; leading prosperous farmers may accumulate wealth and prestige by mining the soil. They advocate "Get all you can while the getting is good." The temperance society, the pastors, the deacons, and parents say "Do not drink," and the billboards, the saloons, the movies, and magazines say "Boys, it's a great thing to drink; all the leading people do it." The church says "Live by the Spirit; the best and greatest values of life are spiritual," while the community puts a premium on material advance.

All leaders of experience recognize the difference in communities. In one it is five times easier to win people to the good life than in others. Some communities seem possessed of evil. Some endowed with goodness elevate each oncoming generation. What the total community is has a profound educative effect on each agency in the community, on each person.

The community may be responsible for juvenile delinquency or for juvenile development. If judges named the real culprit, in some instances, the community would go to jail. Some are redeemed to noble living because of what the community is.

So, the church must be concerned with the community, lest it do wrong by the people. If the church is to express itself fully in the lives of individual persons, it must be a transforming agent in the community as a whole. The community must aid and not hinder the church's mission of redemption. When the church and the community, like a team of horses, pull together, the church sees a large harvest of things of the spirit.

To become effective in serving the community, the rural church must face certain problems in its own structure. Their solution becomes imperative as it seeks to be a more effective force. Certain of these problems have to do with ministerial leadership, support for the minister, the minister's tenure, equipment in buildings, and facilities for carrying on the program.

Concerning adequate ministerial leadership for rural churches there is concern at four points: the supply of ministers, their training, the outlook of rural ministers, and the tenure of rural ministers.

There are probably a sufficient number of ministers to supply the churches of the rural section, but when those engaged in secular activities, the untrained, and those otherwise unavailable are eliminated, the supply is not adequate. The shortage of leadership was aggravated during the war through the draining off of ministers to the chaplaincy, the opening of positions for special religious service, the greater demand in city churches, and the tempting offers in secular occupations. Those concerned with helping churches find pastors are aware of the acute shortage of qualified ministers.

By most standards, an adequately trained minister has had four years of college and three years of seminary training. While some communions have achieved remarkable success in keeping the standards up, others have no recourse but to open the gates to untrained men.

Even as serious is the dearth of ministers with specific training for rural service. This training is desirable because of the need for ministers to be conversant with the resources, methods, and programs appropriate to the rural situation. Rural church training programs are still in their infancy. Not many pastors have availed themselves of adequate courses of this type.

The attitudes and outlook in the rural ministry are not reassuring. There is a restlessness, a feeling that the field of service is not challenging, that other positions offer improved status, that the city church is preferable. The causes of this lack of eagerness are many and deep-seated.

The tenure of rural pastors is short. John Frederic Oberlin's example of a fifty-nine-year pastorate has not been and is not the American pattern. In some states there is a turnover in rural parishes on an average of once every two years. The facetious remark that a minister doesn't place a setting of eggs under a hen for fear he will have moved before they are hatched carries a measure of truth.

An investigation among a number of rural ministers and their wives reveals some of the reasons for short pastorates. These are given here as they were spoken.

Ministers by the end of three years have given all they have to give and, having stopped growing, acquire no new resources. . . . Churches have a tradition of short pastorates and become restless after a pastor has been on the field a year or two. Some churches take the heart out of a man. One church votes on the pastor each year, usually voting him out. . . . The rural fields are so difficult that a pastor unable to make an impression soon wearies and seeks a new field. . . . The minister's wife may not like the church or does not appreciate the rural ministry or becomes discouraged over the unattractive, uncomfortable, poorly equipped parsonage. A minister's wife was told, "We used to wash by hand. You can do it the rural way." The lack of educational facilities, especially high school, family sickness, remoteness from hospitals and doctors, and the burden of medical bills are further reasons for moving. . . . The denominational supervisory setup is not equipped to give counsel and help in a crisis, and the pastor does not have resources to weather it. . . . The pastor sees a field that is more desirable.

Probably the principal reason of all is that pastors fail fully to grasp the length and breadth and height of the Christian ministry and do not conceive a program required to carry out this ministry. Obviously the church cannot be a community-serving institution with a rapid turnover in leadership. The time required to know the community, the slowness of the educative process, the time element in bringing about change are such as to call for longer pastorates.

Closely related to the short tenure of pastors is the matter of salary. We have noted that the minister is expected to have seven years of training after high school, and additional specialized training is advised. That is within four years of the period of training required to be a doctor of medicine. It is more training than a high school principal generally has. It is considerably above that received by the teachers and other professional people.

Yet, the minister receives a salary that is a mere pittance compared to the income of the doctor, and lower than the salary of the extension agent and the high school principal. He often is among the poorest paid public servants in rural society. Yet, potentially, he is the most useful community leader.

The minister does not expect his income to match that of the doctor, the lawyer, the dentist, the veterinarian, the banker, and many small town business men and farmers. But, until he can receive an income that will provide the minimum basic needs, comforts, conveniences, and securities, the rural church will have a serious problem in retaining leadership. The problem is more pressing to the church concerned for the welfare of the whole community.

A group of ministers and laymen stated that the income of a pastor needs to be large enough to provide "adequate ministerial support." This presupposes the practice of economy on the part of the pastor and his family, but should make reasonable provision for:

Material needs: food, clothing, comfortable housing, fuel, light, water, and telephone.

Cultural needs: books, magazines, conferences, schools, and education of children.

Health needs: doctor and dentist bills, etc.

Traveling expenses: payment for use of car — mileage basis or flat sum.

Giving: including the many calls for financial help that come to the minister.

Saving: for emergencies and old age, through insurance and minister's pension plans.

Office expense: postage, stationery, printing, office equipment, should be cared for by the church apart from the pastor's salary.

The need for good facilities for the church is more obvious than ever before. People are accustomed to a higher standard of public service, they are accustomed to centralized schools, and they see examples of architectural excellence in modern post offices, filling stations, and drive-in markets. Equipment of many kinds is available to a degree never attained before. The church people expect more from the church than ever before. Added together, these conditions make a demand that the church have added facilities.

Among the tens of thousands of buildings there are many that are inadequate as to size, facilities, equipment, and architectural soundness. Many one-room buildings are arranged for preaching and for little else. Other buildings are architectural monstrosities that do not represent the purpose of the church. Again, churches are unattractive outside and inside, and poorly kept.

More systematic information is available about rural parsonages since Professor Ralph A. Felton made a study of 1,171 parsonages. Some churches have beautiful, modern parsonages. On the debit side, Professor Felton estimates that of the 100,000 parsonages in the United States, about 40,000 are seriously in need of improvement. He quotes a survey made by a student that demonstrates that the ministers' wives are often the best educated women in the community. These women who give their lives without salary ought to have good homes in which to live, he concludes.

Similarly, the minister's study needs to have facilities measured in terms of comfort, convenience, equipment, and library.

With the extension of electricity to many parts of the country the use of added equipment is made possible. Electric organs, audio and visual aids (including money for film rental and screens), record players, and wire recorders are among forms of equipment desired. Gowns for the choir, music for the choir and organ, standard hymnals, appropriate works of art — these are as invaluable to a rural church program as to the city church. The modern church needs to be equipped with facilities for worship, education, sociability, and recreation.

A small competitive church without community outlook cannot afford an adequate building with rooms for all purposes and a modern parsonage with study. Indeed, it doesn't need them. They are too big a load on the people. To the community-minded church they become imperative. A great work demands good facilities: equipment that encourages the growth of the cause, tools that symbolize the exalted tasks of the church.

This concern of the church may be summarized: to perform its greatest service in the community it needs a minister who is highly trained, supported at a level adequate for modest but comfortable living and given equipment adequate in convenience, appearance, appropriateness, and extent to do the work. The noblest work on earth is done sacrificially and devotedly but with good instruments.

References

1. From an article by Ben Crouch, in *Successful Farming*, August, 1948, p. 26. Used by permission.
2. "I Believe," by Ralph L. Williamson, in *New York State Christian Rural Fellowship Bulletin*, Number 12, October, 1938, p. 1. Used by permission.
3. Don F. Pielstick, in reporting a study of Douglas County, Illinois, indicates that about half (49.8 per cent) of the people in the county live in seven incorporated places. Seven churches in centers of 1,000 to 2,000 population reported only 31.3 per cent of their members drawn from the open country. "Since the membership of these 11 churches represents 77.5 per cent of all church members reported, it would seem to indicate that the open country is not being as adequately cared for as the town or the village. Apparently, far and wide, the churches are neglecting the people who live in the outer circle geographically." — "A Study of Protestant Churches in Douglas, Hancock, and Whiteside Counties, Illinois, 1947," by Don F. Pielstick. New York, Committee on Cooperative Field Research of the Home Missions Council of North America.
4. "The number of church members reported by the pastors of the rural churches as living on farms was 34 per cent of the population living on farms (1940 census); the number of church members reported by the pastors as not living on farms was 52.6 per cent of the village and non-farm open country population." — "The Mission of the Rural Church," by William G. Mather. New York, the American Baptist Home Mission Society, 1948. Used by permission.
5. P. 23. Madison, N. J., Felton, 1947. Used by permission.
6. See pp. 159 and 160 for further information about Oberlin's ministry.

CHAPTER 4

The Church's Rural Strength

As the Allenville Community Baptist Church in Wisconsin approached its one hundredth anniversary, some of the members thought its days were numbered. Five other churches within a radius of five miles had died in that century and this was the only one remaining. It did not adequately support the pastor, and its circle of outreach was contracting. How long it could hold out was anyone's guess.

But prospects were brighter at Allenville than most supposed. Two youthful pastors and their wives became immediately responsible for the church's taking on new life.

One by one they added new elements and vitality to the program. The young married couples' club revived. A parish paper carried a message into each home monthly. A reporter wrote up events for the Oshkosh newspaper. Stewards were appointed for the pastoral supervision of the people in the area in which each lived.

By the time of the one hundredth anniversary celebration the church was again vigorous. The celebration was planned so the people would look back in order that the church might go forward. The emphasis was upon "beginning the second hundred years."

Improvements were undertaken. The church basement was painted and an oil-burning hot-air furnace installed. Screens were purchased to divide classes. A complete rebuilding and repainting of the basement were later undertaken. Fluorescent lights were installed.

The parsonage, too, came in for improvements: a costly deep well, redecorating, and fuel-saving insulation. The minister invested additional time and dollars to make the parsonage attractive and useful with a study and facilities for church meetings of various kinds. The pastor and his wife say that a good parsonage is the best kind of "minister insurance." It keeps him on the field.

All the improvement was done with the purpose of making the church effective in reaching and serving people. A graded Sunday school, a class for training in church membership, socials, and many other activities were intensified. New people were won to church membership.

Symbolic of the church's enterprise was the discovery of and ministry to Butte des Morts. This hamlet about four miles away is located on the shores of a lake. It is made up of a permanent population and the summer people. The year-round residents probably number three hundred. An old church had been abandoned. Some of the people attended church elsewhere, but most stayed at home on Sunday. This applied to the thirty children in the grade school and to the young people attending the Winneconne high school. Many of the parents took no interest in the children's religious needs. The several taverns gave evidence of the nature of the local social and recreational life.

When the Allenville church discovered Butte des Morts, it did not wait long to make a decision. The people in this hamlet did not all have cars. Only a few of those who did would take the trouble to come to church. A bus was the answer.

The bus cost money — $6.00 a week — more than the Allenville church had. But, since a bus was needed, a bus was hired to carry from fifteen to thirty children and young people of high school age to church and Sunday school.

The church bus is symbolic of the solution to this church's problem. It needed a bigger field. It needed a bigger church to operate successfully. A little exploring resulted in the discovery of an area of outreach. The secret of growth is that this church pushed its influence outward instead of letting discouragement or lassitude close in the circle of its parish. If the attitude and trend of the past few years is continued, this church will indeed be larger in numbers and influence in its second century than in the first.

WHAT THE CHURCH MEANS TO PEOPLE

Effective churches mean a good deal more in town and country than people readily express. One townsman said that his church had done some fine things in the community. It had set a pace for the other churches. A farmer's wife declared that Sunday wasn't Sunday without the church service. Both these persons had received much more than that from their lifelong association with the church. By probing a little deeper one comes to see some of the more basic contributions of the church.[1]

The following is a testimony to the church's role as carrier of eternal forces:

There is something inherently impressive about a small voluntary association of Americans which has lasted for a century and a half. When membership in such a group is open to all persons of kindred purposes without distinction of sex, race, age, economic condition, esthetic taste, or degree of education; when it elects its own officers freely and fairly; when it faces the facts of human life yet holds to ideals not generally popular nor easy of achievement; and when, despite its changing personnel it manifests, over the years, a singular power of renewal from within — then it is truly worthy of public celebration.

Reflection upon these matters may indeed suggest the imperishable significance of idealistic groups at a time when measurement technique, mass action, mechanical proficiency, quantity production, military force, and commercial aggression appear to hold the reins of power. Might it be that groups of free persons, motivated by the spirit of Jesus, living in little, friendly communities, still hold the key to human destiny? Such groups do well to believe in themselves as carriers of eternal forces; to reaffirm the validity of their central convictions; and to take courage as they go forward into the unpredictable future.[2]

No two people would agree exactly on the basic needs that a church meets for individuals and society. We shall examine four of the principal contributions under the headings morality, culture, fellowship, and sense of God.

The rural church inspires its members to practise *high moral standards*. To this end it takes leadership in driving evil out of the community. Church leaders are foes of saloons, gambling dives, and houses of ill-fame. Church people do not want their lads playing pool in a parlor that opens into a saloon.

The church takes a positive stand for good morality. Members are expected to be temperate, honest, considerate, helpful, without malice, practising self-control and maintaining a life of chastity.

The results of the church's efforts are often obvious. Divorce, juvenile delinquency, and adult crime are rare in rural communities having a strong church. Unlocked doors and farms left without guard over field and flock are testimonies to the influence of rural churches. The word of most rural people is as good as gold. Even the community liar does not do too much harm, for the people learn to know the truth in his lying.

Thieves are likely to be from a town or city where they hide
among numbers. Those who observe communities widely are
convinced that the level of morality is definitely higher in
places where the church is strong than in those places where it
is weak or nonexistent.

Churches raise people's appreciation of *culture*, of things
good, beautiful, and true. Happily schools, 4-H Clubs, Home
Bureau Community Clubs, and other groups are also fostering
an appreciation of the practical and fine arts. These agencies
often excel the church in this cultural leadership. For instance,
a school may celebrate Christmas with music and a spirit of
reverence more expressive of the message of Christmas than
does the church. Actually, the appreciation of art and cultural
things on the part of the community agencies can be and often
is a boon to the church.

But it is difficult to overestimate the church's influence on
culture. The emphasis upon Sunday as a day set apart produces
several contributions. For instance, the people dress up. The
Sunday clothes habit can be overdone, but when done in
moderation it lifts morale, enjoyment, and behavior. Sunday
affords freedom to enjoy associations. This includes the development of the art of conversation, discussion in a class or society,
table comradeship, the art of entertaining guests, and numerous
other graces. It provides time to take an appreciative attitude
toward the home, the farm, the community. The fields take on
a different color to the boy freed from work on Sunday.

Crévecoeur, who immigrated to America in 1765, observed
that among the early settlers there was a tendency to degenerate.
They seemed to retain the vices of Europeans and in addition
adopted some from the Indians. In this situation, writes Crévecoeur, "The Sunday meetings, exclusive of religious benefits, were the only social bonds that might have inspired them
to some degree of emulation in neatness." [3] There are many

other forces in modern life to call people from barbaric habits, attitudes, and appearance, but Sunday is one of the strongest forces of all.

In considering the cultural contributions of the church, one cannot overlook the influence of its literature, hymnology, and forms of worship. Many a rural person who would never pause for a moment with Shakespeare pores over the pages of the Bible, becoming familiar with the most exalted literature of all time. Men and women without learning, as well as those with it, memorize passagas of Scripture. In prayer they frequently use language more discriminately and beautifully than is expected of common people. The hymns of the church are noble poetry. Even when churches prefer to sing timely songs and choruses they also choose some that are inspiring and worshipful. The form of service, the attitude of reverence, architectural forms, and the symbolism of the church all raise cultural appreciation.

The church in town and country is strong in *fellowship.* The lives of people become closely knit into the fabric of relationships that are formed in the church. A young man growing up in an open-country church discovered that it offered him more opportunity for comradeship than any other place. The church became the center of his life. It took precedence over everything except the home.

On Sunday morning he attended Sunday school with boys of his own age. The half dozen gave some range for the forming of friendships. At church he sang in the choir or sat in the congregation. He knew every person by name. After-church visiting was as much a part of the day as was the service itself. On Sunday afternoon the visiting back and forth was usually with church families. On Sunday evening the young people's meeting and the evening service brought the youths together. During the week choir rehearsals, sometimes orchestra rehearsal, and an occasional party gave variety to the contacts. Sunday afternoon rehearsals, Christmas exercises, annual picnics, a New Year's Eve social and religious celebration — these all helped to tie his emotional and cultural life to the church.

This young man and his friends felt at home in the church. It was the place to which they belonged. They were helped by the sermons, the lessons, the discussions, and the prayers. They were held by the comradeships. The church was the best place in the whole community. It was a place where one counted as a person.

Christian fellowship always has power. The early church had its greatest influence when the people were in a spirit of unity. One of Paul's constant concerns was that the churches that he established enjoy a fellowship of a high order. He saw that fellowship made people want to be together; it relieved people of boredom; it gave support to new converts in living the new life; it had teaching power; it drew others. That is always true of Christian fellowship.

This sense of belonging grows more intense through the years. It is particularly strong in older people. To the unmarried and the widow whose home ties are broken by death or removal, the church may become a sort of larger family. The minister, the church service, the building, the organizations, and classes may be the symbol of it.

But most of all the church points people to *God*. That is its great specialty. That is the focus of all that the church does. Men find God without a church, but the church is made up of people who have found enough in God to want others to have him more fully. It might be called the association of seekers after God.

The church teaches that there cannot be anything worth while in life unless its center and meaning is in God. To know God and love God sincerely is the highest good.

The ways in which the church teaches about God are numerous. The Bible is the God-centered book. Christ is the revelation of God. His church through the ages gives witness. Every hymn is directed to God. The anthems magnify him. The church steeples that rise graceful and high are material symbols of the soul's aspiration toward God. The hush of a communion service, the mystery of worship, the reverent prayers of the devout — these are avenues to God. Even the cemetery once known as God's Acre reminds men that life can have its end in God.

The church helps people to a hope that life is not stopped by death. The grave is not the completion of life. This life here lived in God can be continued more gloriously. Not that people can know how it will happen, but that it *will* happen! The church helps people to believe that life has great possibilities on both sides of Jordan.

The church has more strength to make these contributions when it carries on a *life-centered or comprehensive ministry.* Far from being a new idea, this conception of the church's ministry is deeply ingrained in Christian history. In fact, it had its beginnings among the Hebrews. Along with the teachings about man's relation to God and man's relation to man in general, there were many specific religious precepts. These dealt with an employer's relation to his servants, with working conditions, the use and conservation of land, sanitation and diet, social practices, marriage customs, relationship with foreigners, "social security" for the poor and the aged, and legal procedures. The religion of the Hebrews permeated the everyday needs and affairs of the people. It was not a one-day-a-week or a one-phase-of-life affair.

So it was with the ministry of Jesus. It has been said, "Jesus came living: working, being friendly, cooperating, health-building, studying, teaching, recreating, worshiping, preaching, witnessing — activities never separated from life, facets of one purpose, phases of one process." [4]

Freshly influenced by Jesus, the early Christians at Jerusalem carried on in much the same way. This church prayed, worshiped, preached, had fellowship, baptized, taught, shared economically, healed, ministered to the widows and others in need, and engaged in missionary outreach. The program was as extensive as the needs of the people were acute.

No church can thrive with a lesser ideal. Modern methods will vary from what they were in primitive situations, but the impulse to service is the same. Such a conception of program will not send a church on a wild spree of unthinking activity. It will help it carefully and prayerfully to consider what its business is in the community.

The potential of the rural church needs to be understood and reckoned with by the church at large. It has been seen that the rural church has made a contribution far greater than would be recognized by those who see it only outwardly. It has had a stronger hold on the lives of people than any other influence except that of the home. Yet, too commonly, the people in rural churches are not fully conscious of their own power and potentiality. The community-conscious church needs to be aware of both.

The church deals with people through their life span. It shares this characteristic with the home. The school, with all its helpfulness, works only with children from five to eighteen or nineteen years of age. The church puts babies on the cradle roll and names them in prayer. They are dedicated or baptized at an early age. Often they are carried to church in the mothers' arms. Nurseries are provided. At an early age children attend Sunday school, from which they need never graduate short of death. The church offers youth activities and nurtures many a courtship. It elevates and blesses the union of man and maid in marriage. It dedicates homes. It stands by the adults through their years of maturity and does not forget them in their sunset years. When death comes the church is at hand to give assurance.

The church works with families more than does any other institution. It looks upon the home as the institution that has a divinely ordained privilege and opportunity to train for living. It encourages spiritual exercises, ideals, and practices of various kinds to strengthen the home. The church provides the family pew, the family fellowship night, picnics, and home meetings.

The church deals with generations. It recognizes that life loses all its color and significance if it has only a present. A man must be rooted in a past; he must have a future. Life, each life, is a part of God's eternity. It grows out of a long tradition. It will be projected into the future for good or for ill. In the church one feels, "O Lord, thou hast been our dwelling place in all generations. Before the mountains were brought forth. . . ." One sees the vision of a new heaven and a new earth. One feels the pulse of eternity. By its architecture, remembrance plaques, memorials, hymns, services, and scriptures the church quickens the people to see their place in eternity.

It has long been recognized that the rural setting is advantageous to the growth of spiritual qualities in the lives of individuals. From the earliest days men found God through natural phenomena. Jacob, Moses, and the Psalmists illustrate this. Recent students of national life are aware of this contribution of the rural setting to character. There is a relation between religion and agriculture. The nearer agriculture comes to dealing with the natural forces, the stronger are these influences. The miner who digs coal, especially if he digs for others in mass effort, is further removed from some of the influences than the man who sows seed.

The mystery of the seed, the miracle of reproduction in plant and animal, the coming of storms, the salubrious weather, the march of the seasons, the panorama of nature's artistry in form and color — these are among the natural forces that turn a man to wonder and search for a Creator God.

Then, too, the intimate nature of rural life develops a sense of responsibility that issues in the sturdy qualities of integrity of character and helpfulness.

Charles Galpin, noted as a sociologist, writes, "The Old Testament is a joint book of country life and religion. The Psalms breathe the free spirit of the winds. The hills, the streams, the pastures and meadows, the grass and the grain are all there. . . . The parables of Jesus are in the language of the field and farm work . . . the sheep and the shepherd, the tares, the vine and its branches, the wicked husbandman. The language of mystery, growth, and decay will doubtless always be agricultural. The ancient farmer and the modern farmer seem linked indissolubly to religion." [5]

To suppose that the rural church is automatically strong is a serious error. The resources are available. The prospects are bright. But they are like the majesty of a sunrise, available only to those who see.

WHAT CAN BE DONE WITH LITTLE CHURCHES?

If the rural church's strength is to be developed, there needs to be some candid and straight thinking about the small church. Key laymen, as well as ministers and administrators, need to do the thinking, which is necessary because of a conflict between desire and reality. The problem is simple. Rural people want a church to do the work of an institution, although the resources available may be barely enough to support a fellowship.

Rural people habitually organize and try to maintain churches under conditions that defeat the growth of the church of their heart's desire. Their situation is a little bit like that of a child crying for the moon, but without a ladder long enough to reach it. They want large churches without the conditions that work for large churches. It is easier to fashion pews than to fill them. There has been more ardor for organizing churches and erecting edifices than there has been skill in nurturing strong congregations.

The American villages and countrysides are dotted with small neighborhood competitive churches. Many of them had their origin in the horse-and-buggy days. Some are buggy-day churches instituted more recently by automobile-driving adherents. They are the subject of much sentiment.

> I so love little churches!
> Vine-clad, of stone or brick,
> Hid among elms and birches,
> Time-hallowed, gentle places,
> With welcome that embraces
> Both saint and heretic.
>
> Ah, give me little churches
> My happy childhood knew!
> Time-hallowed, gentle places,
> Hid among elms and birches
> Dear little country churches —
> I think God loves them, too.[6]
> — Edith D. Osborne

OVERCHURCHING MAY RESULT IN UNDERSERVING THE COMMUNITIES

A most striking illustration of the churches' inefficiency may be found in southern and southeastern Ohio. Here, in a region covering at least eighteen counties, the failure of the churches may fairly be called pathetic. . . . Although the churches have been here for more than a century, no normal type of organized religion is really flourishing, while the only kind which during the past fifteen years has been gaining ground, the cult of the Holy Rollers, is scarcely better than that of a Dervish. The churches have failed and are failing to dispel ignorance and superstition, to prevent the increase of vice, the spread of disease, and the general moral and spiritual decadence of the people.[7]

From this description, one might infer that the region mentioned was unchurched. Not so! In Monroe County there was one church for every 214 persons; Pike, one for every 211; Gallia, one for 197; Morgan, one for 194; and so on. The worst moral and religious conditions were found where there were the largest number of churches in proportion to the inhabitants. Overchurching and underserving went hand in hand. Resources were so drained in supporting the institution that there was little strength left for doing the work for which it was established.

The program of the little church is apt to be limited. Don F. Pielstick says of the smallest churches, which constitute one-fifth of the total churches in two Illinois counties: "Take a look at what the too-small unit does to the church program. Often the small church is maintained only by a worship service . . . the fifth representing the smallest churches had an average of only 35 at the chief service. Spread this number over the life span — from baby to grandparent — and what kind of an impression of divine worship is being instilled in the children and the youth, and what kind of an appeal is being made to the unchurched?" [8]

Few of the smaller churches have a men's program other than is provided at the principal worship service. The young people fare better but not well enough, and the women do even better. There is a lack in the field of leadership training, in a family ministry, in age-group needs, in music, and in many other areas.

Mr. Pielstick concludes: "These small churches are much

like many small patches of land found on most farms — too small to be cultivated efficiently and too fertile to lie idle." [9]

Contrasted with the 35 churches of one denomination now functioning in an area of another state, 50 others have died. The small church is too much at the mercy of sporadic, irresponsible, independent, untrained leadership. It is subject to ingrown loyalties, to shortsightedness, and lackadaisical ease.

One reason the small church has such a hard time is that the people want the rural church to do the work of an institution, yet supply it only with the resources of a fellowship group. To see the effect of this error on the life of the church let us for a moment turn to the past.

In the early stages of development, churches usually are unorganized fellowships. So it was with the church of which the twelve disciples were constituents. There were no established offices, except that of treasurer, and any specific responsibilities were related to individuals, not to offices. Jesus as leader held his place not by election or heredity, but only through his personal power and his unparalleled ability to draw men about himself. He made no provision for the perpetuation of the group.

The early Jerusalem church was just as informal. In it men and women were bound together in great expectancy of what Christ would do in and through them. This church at first had no officers, no salaried leaders nor servants, no place of worship to be maintained and no rituals to follow.

In the thrust of American population westward one observes again the formation of simple Christian fellowships. No sooner were homes set up on plain or wilderness clearing than the families established common worship. There was no building, no paid minister, and no elaborately established church organization. Meetings were held in groves, homes, barns, or schoolhouses. Today groups such as the Pentecostals and the

Nazarenes are demonstrating anew a type of church with many fellowship qualities.

As these informal groups grow older, certain functions and rites become set. Churches are housed in edifices especially constructed and set apart. These structures have been planted the length and breadth of America; few communities are without one, and many have several spires piercing the sky. Seminaries and Bible schools have been organized for the training of men and women for full-time professional service.

American church people unanimously believe in a church institution with an accepted form of church edifice, a salaried minister, and an established form of organization and ritual. Any suggestion to rural people that they give up a church edifice and the services of a minister is tantamount to asking for the dismemberment of the church. Church executives and administrators make no place at all for a church that cannot be an institution in this accepted sense.

While this setting of organization has been taking place, the environment in which these churches have been planted has been changing. In vast areas the change has brought about a depletion of resources upon which the church depends for its existence. Where the changes have been most rapid and extensive, the result has been most disastrous.

Students of the rural church have analyzed the reasons for this disintegration. Decline and shifts in population, the economic disadvantage of the rural people, the increased cost of church maintenance, the disappearing neighborhood, and secularism are commonly named causes. But, in one sense, these are not first causes. The rural church could carry on without casualty despite these conditions. *These forces work havoc because the country church attempts to remain unchanged in an environment with declining resources.* Its leaders have been slow to recognize this.

On the one hand, the informal fellowship group is almost freed from economic and sociological factors. The reasons for this are apparent. Rural America can support as many Christian fellowships as there is spiritual devotion to maintain them. But on the other hand, the church as an institution demands economic and social support, in addition to devotion. The church weakens or dies if it does not have those social and economic elements necessary for its existence.

The rural church may be compared to farming. One of the most widely accepted maxims of the family farm is that it must be large enough for efficient operation. A tractor does not pay for itself on a farm too small. The family does not have enough income; it is deprived of many essentials for living.

The farmer buys additional acres to make his farm reach the efficient size; the doctor figures on enough patients to provide ample income; the merchant thinks in terms of volume. What does this mean to the church? The church, too, needs numbers and income as well as dedication if it is to provide certain desired services and satisfactions.

Another factor has been emerging in rural church affairs: namely, rural church people are expecting more from their ministers. They want fully trained ministers.

A small Kansas community found that a doctor needed $15,000 worth of equipment to start his practice in a small town. They pitched in and raised the money. That highlights the predicament of the trained minister. He wants to go into a situation that provides ample tools and resources for his work. He is a man in earnest. Why did he devote himself to seven years of study and discipline? He doesn't expect a doctor's income. He does want a challenging field. He wants to build Christ into the community. He doesn't care to compete with other small churches. He doesn't want to give his life as a private chaplain to a few people. He is prepared and eager to lead the church in becoming a strong force in the community. A minister can no more accomplish his purposes and the purposes of God by ministering solely to forty families, saints and sinners, than can a doctor. He rises to a challenge.[10]

We are now ready to raise the question: *How large a population is required to support a church?* Many years ago, the Home Missions Council estimated that on the average there should be one church for every thousand population. The thousand would give adequate support and permit a broad program and provide good facilities. Everyone knows that in exceptional instances, fewer people than that support a church. A few consecrated, generous people can do more than many disinterested people. Yet experience proves the wisdom of the above estimate. Now some rural leaders are raising the estimate: one Protestant church for 1,500 people; one for a rural community. As people's notion of what a church should provide expands, the number of people necessary to support a church increases.

This reasoning apparently has brought us to an impasse. Small neighborhood churches are vulnerable; they have excessive problems. The rural church must be a larger church. That is one way to increase its effectiveness.

Consolidation is one apparent means of having the larger church. "Close the little churches; the people can go to town." That note has been sounded since the advent of the automobile and good roads. In some instances that has been the answer. The general trend is that way. But the road ahead is not so plainly laid out.

Consolidation will not in itself answer the situation. It has been noted that rural people in particular want their church to be intimate. People are not interested in the church that would take them too far out of their neighborhood, depriving them of informal fellowship. That is where the advocates of consolidated churches have erred. They thought that because there are good roads all people would naturally drive to the centers for religious contacts.

There are countless instances of the survival or revival of neighborhood groups. A hill neighborhood book club may serve as the integrating force for a group thought dead. Though only three miles from town, these people do not attend the town church.

Wisconsin rural sociologists, after exhaustive research, point out that the neighborhoods are persisting. In Virginia the same is true. In a New Hampshire hamlet, the church has died, but the Grange remains strong. Two and a half miles out an informal Saturday night club brings fifteen to thirty neighbors together for sociability and discussion. The neighborhood is not dead. Very frequently people want it as the basis of their church life.

Moreover, neighborhood churches have much to contribute to their own populations and to the nation. They often are filled with children and young people. New members in these churches come by baptism. In the towns and cities more come by transfer. They provide a fellowship unsurpassed for warmth and enthusiasm. Ash Ridge, Green Hollow, or Turkey Hill may not have many people, the program may be limited, the out- look restricted, but the church is about the brightest spot in the neighborhood. Close all the neighborhood and too-small churches in the land and the spiritual and moral foundations of the nation are threatened.

These two trends toward centralization and toward neighbor- hood grouping seem contradictory. It seems that we cannot have one without losing the other. The answer to the rural church problem demands that we have both. How can we have both? If the rural community is to be served effectively, the church must candidly face this question.

Let us examine various forms of rural church cooperation to see whether or not they suggest an answer to the problem. At least four characteristics will be seen to apply to this question.

(1) Many forms of church cooperation are indigenous; they evolve locally to meet conditions in various situations.

(2) Each one of these forms of organization gives the church a larger constituency. The direction is definitely and invariably in the direction of a larger rural church.

(3) Most forms of cooperation take into account the small church and group. The small unit is not overlooked. This is particularly true in the larger-parish type of organization.

(4) There is a widespread practice of various forms of interchurch cooperation, and a considerable body of information about the experience of the churches is available. Those desiring to inaugurate an interchurch ministry need not experiment blindly. *Town and Country Church*, a periodical for rural ministers, regularly carries accounts of what churches are doing and how they are doing it. Professor Ralph A. Felton at Drew Theological Seminary, Madison, New Jersey, repeatedly has studied cooperative churches and has published the findings.

IS COOPERATIVE ORGANIZATION THE ANSWER?

Churches everywhere that are imbued with the community spirit are interested in adjusting their organization to meet the needs of the community. Reorganizing for cooperative action outwardly appears to be formal and routine. Actually, it is exciting and pioneering. Young ministers leading people to reorganize for effective service act like men reborn. Groups of twenty to fifty persons wrestling with the reorganization of churches for community redemption are as eager as New Testament Christians. Wherever cooperative organization grows out of a new sense of mission and a compulsion to serve and unite the community, the gospel of Christ takes on new power. On the contrary, where the organization is routine and an end in itself, there is not more life than in any sleepy church.

The Inter-Church Council is one effective form of cooperative organization. Here is an example of how it works: Corona is a town of 2,200 people, plus those in the surrounding territory. Among the six churches were three old-line Protestant churches located in close proximity. Each church had a pastor and each had a program. There was ordinary good will. For many decades there was occasional cooperative effort. In the late 1910's some of the people and pastors thought essential cooperative activities warranted a central organization. An Inter-Church Council was established, with its membership composed of the pastor and two representatives from each church.

In that town the three churches embarked on a program that has been maintained and increased through the years. The Inter-Church Council sponsored joint surveys, evangelistic services, Sunday school enlargement programs. The Sunday morning bellringing was coordinated to an interringing system that the janitors devised. Thanksgiving services, Holy Week services, and Sunday evening services were added. Later there came vacation Bible schools, week-day religious education, youth meetings, and other activities.

The Inter-Church Council has had a generation of experience. Some people think that the three churches ought to get together in one Protestant church with a staff of specialists. Most want to keep their own separate churches, but they are convinced that many activities should be carried on together. The Inter-Church Council is a means of doing that. It also provides a means for arriving at a common policy on matters affecting all the churches. It is a symbol of the desire of the churches to serve and unite the community.

That type of organization has been established in many communities and it is widely approved and accepted. It has made a large contribution to the spiritual life of the communities.

The Inter-Church Council frequently has some blind spots that limit its full effectiveness. It has been too little conscious of the community ideal. It has not gone far enough in integrating the efforts of the church in serving community needs. Frequently its interest stops at the village or town boundaries. It is a town-minded body, usually neglecting to bring the churches in the larger community into its thinking and membership.

COUNCILS OF CHURCHES

When the people in *Dundee, New York*, and in the surrounding hamlets and open country decided to centralize their schools, they brought together about 800 pupils. Fifteen buses make the daily rounds, bringing children in and taking them home again. The centralized school is the largest social institution ever established in the area, and is bringing about some far-reaching changes.

The churches almost immediately saw an opportunity to provide Christian instruction on a scale never before dreamed possible. The village churches employed a woman teacher of religion. Since the children benefiting came from the country as well as from the village, some of the country churches were assessed. They responded without objection, although they did not share in planning the program.

Some of the village religious leaders soon saw that all the churches should be "in on the planning as well as on the paying." Again there was an answer. Each church in the area was asked to name representatives on a council that would plan cooperative activities. Nine churches responded, three in the village and six in the surrounding countryside. Four denominations were represented, seven ministers and eighteen laymen making up the council.

This new organization is called the Dundee Area Council of

Churches. It has a president, a secretary, a corresponding secretary, and a treasurer.

The Dundee council has a growing program, although it was organized only in 1948. The teacher is trained and she is paid a salary. In the course of a week about 250 pupils are shuttled by bus from the school to the churches for these classes. (The Roman Catholic children are taught by their priest.)

Vacation church schools will be held not only at the center, but in certain hamlets and open-country churches. The vacation schools can operate best when decentralized, but there is common planning, organization, and training of leaders.

Union services call for a united Thanksgiving meeting in Dundee and for special union services held in the churches of the surrounding area.

A Cub Scout program is contemplated. Den mothers have been enlisted to lead the dens in the hamlets as well as at the center. An annual approved leadership training program is available to all the teachers in the churches that make up the council.

The collection taken at union services goes into the common treasury to support the council program.

This council of churches is doing through the churches spiritually what the centralized school is doing for the area educationally. They are working together to provide a better service for all the people. The churches are doing more than that. They are helping to build a new and larger community in this district of about a hundred square miles populated with three to four thousand people. The churches are seeking to provide the spiritual ingredients that go into the making of the good community. The neighborhoods and the open country are finding a new focus in the center. The business of the churches is to lead each person to God. It also sees these people coming into a new dimension of living by building the structure of a new community on solid spiritual foundations.

The community church is another cooperative form. There are few words that have held more charm for more rural people than the term *community church*. Particularly in small neighborhoods without long church tradition it is commonly said, "We need a community church." What is really meant in most instances is, "We want a church that is open to everyone, that serves all the people, and that doesn't divide the community."

It was that desire that gave rise to the community church movement that started after the turn of the century. The same interest continues today. Here is how it happened. A number of people moving west into Montana were faced with the need for a church. They were small in number and were of several denominational backgrounds. They were also realistic. They knew their town would not grow much. At any rate, there was room for only one church. Even that could not be supported as they liked. No one denomination predominated. The leaders wanted to be fair to all, so they decided to organize a community church. Members of any evangelical denomination could join. New converts had a choice as to form of baptism. The church had no outside connection with any denomination. The minister could belong to any denomination or to none. The church's missionary contributions were used to support such projects as the people chose. There was complete freedom from ecclesiastical control. There were no visits by a district missionary, a state executive, or a representative of a national board.

This was a movement of the people. The church belonged to the community. It was a revolt against competition. Some saw in it a fulfillment of the prayer of Jesus that all might be one.

The community church movement spread. Churches were formed in all parts of the country, no one knows how many. A national organization or association was formed and a paper was published.

The community church has given a great deal to the rural church movement. It has pointed out the evils of competition. It has upheld a vision of service and unity in the community. It has stirred the hearts and hopes of many people. It has developed some strong, spiritually powerful churches.

The community church has not generally been dynamic and successful. One reason is that community church leaders have leaned over backward in trying not to become another denomination. No seminaries have been established. There has been little indoctrination of church members with the aims and purposes of a community church. Churches have difficulty in finding ministers competent and sympathetic. There has been a narrowing of world horizons. Churches facing trouble or opportunity have suffered for lack of counsel. Some churches are narrow as well as provincial. Others are too much like the community — worldly.

The community church is still a factor in rural America, but its influence is mostly in the ideals that inspired it rather than in its effectiveness and extent.

The denominational community church may be described as a community church that is associated with some denomination. Or, it may be said to be a denominational church that has been infused with the community church idea to such an extent that it opens its membership to all Protestant Christians.

The formation of denominational community churches comes from a two-way movement, from community churches that feel the need of association with a denomination and from denominational churches eager to serve all the people in the community.

In some churches the members are mostly affiliated with one denomination, with only a few from other denominations. The membership composition in others is like a patchwork quilt with only a few blocks of any one color.

These churches aim to serve the community. They provide fellowship for Christians of various faiths. They tie the church into an ongoing world-wide missionary program and provide for supervision and leadership.

Because there are so many gradations of membership arrangements, no one has ever tried to count these churches. We do know that their number is increasing, that there are thousands of them, that they are native to new communities and on the increase in old ones.

Many denominational officials who frown upon the unattached community church look with favor upon these churches.

The advance toward the denominational community church has been dogged by the ubiquitous sin of adulteration or mislabelling. Churches have found it difficult to restrain themselves from capitalizing on the popularity of the word "community." So, there are denominational churches that to become community churches have only enlisted a volunteer painter to letter the name on the bulletin board. These churches are willing to take others into membership, but do not otherwise change the church structure to accommodate them.

The federated church is native to the smaller eastern village. It is two or more churches working together as one church.

The federated church has been called the married church. The analogy is apt where two churches come together. Two have united to be one; yet each remains distinct. However, as many as three or more churches may federate.

One can best understand the federated church by looking into a community where one has been formed. There is one church outwardly, but there may be two or more buildings once occupied by the formerly separate congregations. Within the one church are separate denominational units that support their own missionary program and keep relationship to their headquarters. There is one pastor and one program.

In central New York there is a community of 900 population in a village and surrounding territory that had two churches, a Baptist and a Presbyterian. They had over a hundred years of history in the 1920's, but things were not going too well. A federation was suggested and the plan carried through. The depression years that followed were not easy, but nevertheless the federated church came through to an ever enlarging strength and service. A new building was dedicated in 1948. The people are enthusiastic about the two-in-one church in its new home.

The case for the federated church becomes clearer in more desperate situations. A community with no more than 450 people had five churches, each one reduced to impotence. The movement toward unity led one to close and three to federate. For a generation now, there has been one Protestant federated church and one Roman Catholic church. The fact that no one wants to go back to the old days is a testimony to the place of the united church in the lives of the people and in the community.

The federated church is an attempt to adjust the church organization to the population where there are too many churches for too few people. It is not a substitute for evangelism outreach and hard work. It takes a realistic view of the relationship between the church as an institution and the number of people.

The federated church does not revolt against denominations. It only believes they should work together.

The attitude toward federated churches varies widely and it varies by regions. The Middle West has few and generally has little faith in them; the northeastern states have many and won't give them up. The members of federated churches are happy; otherwise they would vote for a change. Church administrators find working with a federated church quite complicated. Many pastors are highly pleased. They like to maintain the wider contacts offered by the association with more than one denomination. They like to serve all the people in the community. Other pastors object to the complicated church machinery, or don't see how a pastor can serve several groups without sacrificing his own convictions. On the whole, the federated church has turned the tide of religious life in the declining village.

The larger parish merits close attention as another form of cooperative organization. Here is an example of it:

Located in the heart of a beautiful, hilly countryside, an industrial village lies comfortably nestled in the arms of a little valley. That village is well churched — five Protestant churches and one Roman Catholic church. Five outlying neighborhood churches have had checkered careers. Until recently, the largest was having increasing difficulty in keeping the kind of pastor it wanted and needed. The weakest church was closed and the sixty families in the neighborhood were hardly touched by any other church. Another church had summer services. The two others had no regular leadership. There were two rural slum areas. Religious life expressed through the churches was on the way out. Children were found who did not know the meaning of Christmas, and the name of Christ was known only as a curse. There was not a single country church that could employ a minister, and some were so weak they could not pay $100 a year. They were too small, too weak, lacking in vision.

The village churches had shown some interest and helpfulness in the country churches, but any help was irregular and incidental. The aid was too little to save the neighborhood churches from the abyss of despair into which they had fallen.

Some leaders were sensitive to the plight of these people and aware that a pagan hinterland would eventually paganize the village. Through the interest of far-sighted leaders, a meeting of people from the churches was called to discuss what might be done to better the situation. After several months and numerous meetings the people and the churches decided to form a larger parish. Seven of the churches joined. Four pastors and a trained woman worker formed the staff.

These churches did what churches in many parts of the country have done: they remained separate but banded themselves together to do some things cooperatively.

Genuine larger parishes have some common characteristics that are very significant for the advance of the Christian cause in rural areas. The larger parish was born out of an earnest desire to serve the people.

The larger parish in a real sense is the churches' answer to the little church. It gives it importance. It does so by relating it to other churches in its community, by giving it shared leadership, by leading it on the path of adjustment instead of to decline and extinction.

The larger parish is based upon the new, emerging, larger community. It calls upon the churches to cooperate in doing together in their community those things that can be done better together than separately. The community needs the spiritual power that comes from a united impact. It is the counterpart in things religious to the work of the centralized school in education. The larger parish embraces the outlying area as well as the center. It fits the pattern of the community.

The larger parish builds a cooperative structure through which churches in town and country work together. It has an inter-church council on which all of the village and country churches have representatives. The weakest church usually has as many members on the council as the strongest. They have the same voice. There is no "taxation" without representation in the larger parish. The representatives of all the churches plan together in those matters that can be done better together.

The larger parish plans a comprehensive or diversified program. It does this because of the urgency to serve the whole of people's interests. It does it by having a staff of workers, a pastor with assistants or co-workers; a pastor and a woman "director of religious education"; a pastor and trained lay people who give leadership as a labor of love; a pastor enlisting the resources of constructive community agencies.

The larger parish has not been uniformly successful. It has stirred up a storm in the ecclesiastical teapot. There are many reasons for this. It is not easy to get heretofore independent churches to cooperate fully. Some so-called larger parishes are only a number of unrelated churches strung together on the weak thread of a common pastoral ministry. They are "glorified circuits." Since most communities claim churches of several denominations, it is not possible to have a denominational larger parish in these situations. Here they must be interdenominational — a point that often has been by-passed. There have been difficulties in financing, difficulties in staff relations, difficulties with individualistic churches that want to live and let live, and other problems.

But it has made a tremendous contribution to the advance of rural church work. It has done this in three ways: (1) through service to neglected people and enlarged service to all people, (2) by introducing rediscovered principles of church work, and (3) through "its children." The first two points will be enlarged upon in other chapters. We shall here see how the larger parish has influenced other developments.

Not all denominations, churches, and people are prepared to accept the larger parish idea. It is pretty strong medicine for the body of rural religion. But the idea has been tremendously intriguing — the churches of a larger community working together.

Denominations began to adopt the idea. In West Virginia one denomination that claims several hundred small churches worked out a plan for "grouping the churches." Its churches in a natural area are encouraged to get together through a council and a staff or even one minister.

The Disciples of Christ nationally have sponsored the pastoral unity plan. The description of this plan follows almost to a line the statements on the larger parish, excepting that it is denominational. Both these plans can do great good in bringing near-by churches into cooperative action. Both are limited because there are so many communities where all religious forces must work together if there is to be an effective community religious approach.

There are other developments such as regional parishes in which churches in an area more extensive than the larger community cooperate for certain events and programs. Sometimes a trained woman worker is employed to work among the churches of the region.

The Methodist denomination has emphasized the group ministry. Through this plan several ministers located in a county or similar area exchange services and help one another according to the special ability of each. They meet occasionally for planning and fellowship.

The regional clinic brings pastors and laymen from churches in a region together for occasional meeting to discuss programs, receive instruction from "experts," and for comradeship. "Regional parish" and "council of churches" are names for inter-church organizations that cover several communities.

There are hundreds of communities where some part of the larger parish idea is put into practice with good results. The number of simon-pure larger parishes is limited. That is what is to be expected, but the family of its children is growing.

The multi-denominational church has been born in the wake of tremendous population concentrations of the war period. This church is like a denominational community church, ex-

cept that instead of being related to one denomination it is
related to two or more. It is unlike the federated church in that
there are no denominational units in the church.

These are only some of the better known and commonly
accepted forms of church cooperation.

References

1. Professor W. H. Stacey, extension specialist from the Iowa State College,
   says that rural people want to live in communities that have churches.
   After more than twenty years of observation, he is convinced there are
   six major reasons for wanting a church. These are:
   a. Churches help individuals to develop strengthening religious faiths.
   b. Churches supply spiritual incentives for right living.
   c. Churches inititate and support educational programs.
   d. Churches provide opportunity for esthetic enjoyment.
   e. Churches promote neighborly sociability.
   f. Churches make it possible for individuals to function as world
      citizens. — *Town and Country Church*, September, 1948, p. 13.
2. Speech by Richard H. Edwards, from *The Lisle Congregational Church
   — One Hundred Fiftieth Anniversary, 1797–1947*. Lisle, New York, 1948.
3. *Letters from an American Farmer*, by J. Hector St. John De Crévecoeur,
   p. 53, Everyman's Library. New York, E. P. Dutton & Co., Inc. Used
   by permission.
4. "The Christian Mission among Rural People," p. 42. Rural Missions
   Cooperating Committee of the Foreign Missions Conference of North
   America, 1945. Used by permission.
5. *Rural Social Problems*, by Charles J. Galpin, pp. 123–124. New York,
   The Century Co., 1924. Copyright, Appleton-Century-Crofts, Inc.
   Used by permission.
6. Used by permission of the Methodist Publishing House. Copyright 1934.
7. *Six Thousand Country Churches*, by Charles Otis Gill and Gifford Pin-
   chot, pp. 12–13. New York, The Macmillan Co., 1919.
8. *Town and Country Church*, September, 1948. p. 8.
9. *Ibid.*
10. The information used in the foregoing was taken from an article in
    the *Baptist Leader*.

CHAPTER 5

Home Missions Looks
to the Community

The Olive Hill Church twenty miles west of Raleigh, North Carolina, is called "the busiest place in the community." One of the planks in its platform of service is cooperation with agricultural agencies in helping the farmers to be faithful stewards, using the land for the good of man and the glory of God. Professor Ralph A. Felton writes of the pastor:

Mr. Hendricks tells his farmers in Sunday sermons that they have been entrusted with the business of looking after God's world, which includes caring for the soil on each farm. This he stresses as a religious duty. He sees scientific agriculture as being simply a part of God's laws which we must obey.

One of Mr. Hendricks' deacons is a district soil conservationist. He helps the farmers make out their soil plans. For cooperating farmers, each farm is mapped, and for each field there is a soil plan. Sixty-eight per cent of the farmers in this parish practise contour plowing; 54 per cent put lime on the soil; 73 per cent fertilize their pasture lands; 52 per cent use terraces. Where the slopes are steeper, strip-cropping is practised. One-fourth of the farmers use check dams. Most of the ponds are stocked with fish. Farm ponds not only hold back run-off water, but give farmers and their families fun and recreation.[1]

Because of the scientific care of the soil and other proved
farm practices, the gross income made by farmers here has increased substantially.

This congregation of nearly six hundred members, with their
beautiful and well equipped church, have made their program
lively and comprehensive by using agency resources.

RURAL ALLIES

When the devout and highly trained John Frederic Oberlin
accepted the call to a mountain parish in the Vosges Mountains
of Alsace, he went out as a Christian minister. So far as we know
he went out to a ministry of preaching, teaching, calling, and
counseling in a traditional manner. Yet it was not long before
Pastor Oberlin saw that the avenues through which people
were won to Christ and the means by which Christian people
ministered were many. In the fifty-nine years of his pastorate
he did not neglect the usual and traditional ministries. Many
evidences point to him as a man of far more than ordinary
devoutness. But he was one who could not narrowly confine the
meaning of spirituality.

When Oberlin saw children in a hovel taught by an ignorant
keeper of pigs he did not rest until there were new school buildings and trained teachers using advanced methods. When he
saw people poor and undernourished he experimented with and
introduced better methods of orcharding and raising potatoes.
For the sick he sought medical aid, encouraging young men to
become trained doctors and return to the villages. For the poor
and partially employed he brought in a factory. Seeing that it
was not good to be isolated, he led out in building a bridge and
roads.

Almost singlehanded he carried on a program of such sweeping scope that it was a means of transforming his parish. His
memory has been kept green locally (for 124 years after his

death in 1826 the people still keep flowers on his grave), and he is known to people throughout the world as the beloved Protestant rural saint.

Rural life in the United States has moved out from the period of Oberlin, when the minister was the primary agent for disseminating information, encouraging education, instructing in improved agricultural practices, advising in health matters, and providing for most of the associations among rural people. Today there are many organizations related to rural life that are completely separated from the church. These might be classified as governmental, fraternal and fellowship, and farmers' organizations, and special agencies, institutions, and services. Their number and variety is almost startling, as a glance at the appended list will show.[2]

These can be a tremendous boon to the advancement of the spiritual life of the country. Most of them are conceived with the idea of giving service, and many of them in the spirit of a deep-felt desire to uplift the community. As they keep faithful to their purposes they lengthen the arm of the churches. For instance, the cooperative society for doing business among farmers is so conceived that one of the ablest farm leaders says, "Cooperatives make men." The business of the church is to build men. It can do a better job when its efforts are supplemented by a cooperative that adheres to the high idealism that initiated the movement.

Again, one sees the influence of other community agencies in the program carried on by the public school. For instance, a director of music may teach young people the great music of the past, often the great music of the church. They master instruments in a fashion that astonishes their parents, who have had less opportunity. The moment a program of musical instruction is under way in a school it begins to be reflected in the quality of music in the church. Churches that capitalize on the new skills and appreciation of music enjoy better singing and more inspiring worship services.

In the same way, a home that comes under the influence of a home demonstration agent may raise its standards of sanitation, nutrition, dress, cleanliness, and recreation. These improved conditions, if imbued with what the church has to offer, help to

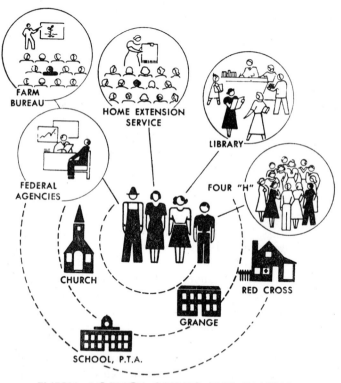

EVERY AGENCY SERVES THE FAMILY

build a family and home whose influence is far-reaching in building the kind of community the church desires.

It suffices to say that there is a deep conviction on the part of many rural church leaders, laymen as well as ministers, that though the problems of the church may be critical, there never before has been a time when the church has had so many allies upon whom to call in the accomplishment of its task.

A common characteristic of these agencies is that, being nonsectarian and dealing with all the people of the community, they make an impact for the growth of community spirit and the emergence of the community.

The church's stake in community agencies and in the outcome of their services and activities is more important than is sometimes supposed. Many agencies carry on exactly the type of service that the church performs under some circumstances. In primitive areas it is the church that sponsors health services, schools, libraries, agricultural leadership, and various other types of economic, social, and cultural activities. The fact that leadership in these activities may reside with some other agency should not cause the church to have less concern for the quality of the service offered. The impact of the agencies upon persons and upon the community as a whole may be just as great as that of the church. The church is as much concerned for "the soul" of a community as for the soul of a person. It is alert as to the quality of the ideals, motives, and behavior of every agency. The church is indeed a shepherd of community agencies. The relationship of the church to the agencies may be compared to that of the leaven to the dough, or, to change metaphor: the church is the light to the community and its agencies, not the community to the church.

There may be said to be three aspects of church and community-agency cooperation. The church may invite agencies to share in church programs and services; the church and agen-

cies may cooperate in joint projects; the church may lend a
hand to agencies in carrying out their programs.

THE CHURCH COOPERATING WITH
COMMUNITY AGENCIES

The minister as leader in community affairs is part of the
church's large contribution to the community. It is a principle
commonly accepted that the minister is a community leader —
that a definite portion of his time is to be given for that purpose.

The well trained minister's experience equips him for community leadership. Because of his acquaintance with community ideals, his wide study and reading, and his general background of training he should know more about planning than
the average citizen.

Meeting with community leaders, sitting with planning
committees, and identifying himself with the constructive
forces are ways in which the minister makes his contribution.

The minister is usually wary of accepting too many offices.
He need not be a "joiner" of every club, lodge, fraternity, and
society that invites his membership. It is possible for him to
become so tied to attendance at meetings that he fails to give
decisive leadership in community or church.

By making the program of the church progressive and constructive, a minister can make one of his most important contributions. A church with such a program will ally itself with
the best in the community and not against it.

Thirty-nine Midwest community-minded ministers discussed the participation of the minister in community life, and
came to the following conclusions:

Half of the group thought that they should participate more in
the community affairs — this in light of the fact that all but five of
them belonged to more than three organizations and one-third of
them to six or more groups. Nearly two-thirds of the group held

offices in organizations other than the church and one-third held
two or more offices. Organizations most frequently participated in
were the PTA, ministerial associations, Boy Scouts (as leaders),
community organizations such as Red Cross, and the Farm Bureau.

Ministers who favored extensive participation in community
activities stated that this was a way of representing the church in
the community, of making it more effective there, and a means by
which a pastor could learn to know his community. The consensus
seemed to be that although community participation was desirable,
it could be overdone. As one person said, "It is wise to be a part of
community activities as much as possible if it is not to the detriment
of the church."[3]

Since the church in general is made up of people of many
social, economic, and theological outlooks, the church neces-
sarily lags behind the convictions and ideals of certain of its
members and even nonmembers. The social adventures that
lead to better forms of social structure must in the very nature of the case be made by a few individuals of unusual insight
or dedication. The wise church encourages or tolerates group
experiments. The ventures may include a prayer or devotional
unit, a group dedicated to world peace, a temperance organization, a credit union, a cooperative society, a labor-capital
coalition group. Such small bodies made up of like-minded persons strongly devoted to certain principles would divide a
church if their activities were brought to the church body for
approval. But the community needs their contribution. If the
church does not give encouragement, who will? The Christian
church grew out of a creative new venture, and this should
inspire more prophetic ventures.

Most churches in town and country have trouble enough in
securing leaders for church responsibilities. How then can one
expect the church to provide leaders for community activities?
That is a question that every church asks. There are several

answers. Some church people will accept community responsibilities more readily than church offices. Those who find new
resources of energy and enthusiasm through community activities may seek service within the church. Persons of Christian character placed in positions of community responsibility
are a means whereby the community and the individuals in it
are helped to be more Christian. That, after all, is the chief
concern of the church.

Community-minded churches have seen opportunities to
serve by making their facilities available at nominal or no cost.
Baby clinics, club meetings, health conferences, demonstra-
tions, farm organization meetings, and scores of other activities are welcomed by churches.

The values of this service are quite evident. A generous
church makes it unnecessary for each agency to purchase buildings or rooms. Where many meetings are held in one place an
investment in superior facilities becomes justified. The church
becomes more central in the thinking of the people as it takes
a natural part in their constructive everyday affairs.

CHARACTERISTICS OF A VITAL COMMUNITY

The church can perform an invaluable service in integrating
the activities and pointing the direction of community agencies.

The Spring Hill Methodist Church in Pennsylvania illustrates admirably the informal cooperation of church and neighborhood agencies.

Spring Hill, Pennsylvania, is a large neighborhood that has
a strong sense of community. It is not a complete community
in itself, but it thinks "our community." Set on the hills and
separated from near-by towns by steep grades, it has maintained a spirit and program that is the pride of the local residents and the talk of many others.

Only a church, a spacious community hall, and a two-room

grade school mark the center of the neighborhood. The area covers about sixteen square miles.

Spring Hill farm land is below average, and the rolling-to-steep hills do not make farming easy. The average elevation of 1,400 feet makes for a shorter growing season and for "rugged" winters.

What is it that has given unusual qualities to this hill neighborhood?

1. The people have an unusual pride in their community. This is evidenced in their concern for the adequate schooling of their children, their willingness to work together for the erection of an attractive and useful community building, and in their support of the church and its program. A young man who grew up in Spring Hill but moved into another community said that one thing he learned at Spring Hill was that "We are individually responsible for the whole group whether we are in a position of leadership or not."

2. There is a cordial welcome to all people to join in the fellowship of community agencies. The 315 people in 70 families living in the area may be classified as old-line stock, new people, and the "unreached newcomers." Ten families now live on land that has remained in the family from the time of the first settlers, and ten more families are descendants of early settlers.

A number of the active leaders have come into the community within the past ten years, some drawn by the wholesome nature of the community life. Also in recent years some of the old farms have been sold to Polish and Italian families with Roman Catholic backgrounds. The unreached group is comprised of families living in poor houses at the edge of the community and families working in town. The hired men and families occupy tenant houses. Their tenure is short.

The community has not been successful in integrating all

the people into the activities of various groups, but new people are received and appreciated. Leaders do have a concern for the unreached.

3. There is deep appreciation of the good life that is available in the community. A farmer's wife said, "I came to this community by chance, but I stayed by choice." One man observed, "There are more people living in this community because they want to than any place I know." Many of the people have developed a philosophy that makes life good to them. Some of the young people feel this and express it when they say there is no particular difficulty in keeping young people interested in the community. Movies in the town, dances, and other attractions do not pull them away from local activities that are provided through the Young People's Society, the Grange, the church, and other agencies. There is no dependence upon the outside for recreation, although the young people and adults do attend the various functions in the high schools at Camptown and Wyalusing. A young man opposed organized Sunday baseball not because it was wrong but because it kept those concerned from the better things the day had to offer.

4. The community has had and continues to have strong lay leadership. The resourcefulness of the leadership is illustrated in a story now woven into tradition.

About a hundred years ago, three farmers driven into the shelter of a barn considered the prohibitive rates charged by insurance companies for fire protection and took steps to organize what is known as the Tuscarora Mutual Insurance Company. The offices of this company are located in a farm home in the Spring Hill community.

On one occasion the Grange was bent on getting every person of voting age to vote in the election. One hundred per cent of the eligible voters went to the polls.

There seems to be a readiness to face tomorrow with an eagerness to do something constructive. Quite frequently in rural communities the young people report that there is no opportunity for expression and leadership. In the Spring Hill community a young man said that he liked to stay in the community because it gave him an opportunity for leadership. The participation of young people and the general regard in which they are held by the elders indicates the truth in the young man's statement.

Some of the leaders are exceedingly busy in community activities. Sometimes it is said that there is too little time for family life. But others point out that among the active families there has not been a serious case of juvenile delinquency or a divorce.

5. The community has a tradition of calling upon outside help for meeting special problems. The State College of Agriculture specialists in soil conservation and progressive farm methods, and local agricultural agents are called upon freely. The extension sociologist is a well known visitor. A conference called in the autumn of 1948 brought several farm, rural life, and rural church specialists into the community.

6. There is a mutual respect and mutual regard for one another in the community. Disagreements in the sense of a variation in points of view are common when programs and projects are under discussion. Yet it is reported that once a decision is made, the people go ahead together.

7. The people's knowledge of how and when to use organization for useful purposes helps to make the community strong. Local organizations seem to elicit great loyalty. For instance, there is a woman's society that reports 100 per cent participation by its members and 90 per cent attendance at monthly meetings. Grange membership is 146, representing 50 families. Yet these organizations pull together.

A young man reported that he is proud of the community because none of its organizations tries to monopolize the time of the people, but allows time for other organizations to make their own contributions. Each agency respects the purpose of the other agencies, thus making a pattern of service.

8. But perhaps most important of all is the church at the center, the most dynamic institution in the community and the hub of activity. Its doors are open to all. It is interested in every constructive activity. It desires the good life for all the people in the community.

The Spring Hill church through informal cooperation with the other agencies gives the religious motive expression in the so-called secular interests. The leaders in the nonchurch organizations boldly state that spiritual values must be at the center of life and that the church is the agency for giving spiritual vitality to the community. This relationship of the church to the agencies is caught up in the remark of a young man, "Our young people have stayed in Sunday school and church because what we do there is related to all we do."

The effective community council represents the ideal in community planning. A community council is made up of representatives from all agencies. As a planning body it unifies and directs the community toward goals. It acts as a clearing house. The following account illustrates its functions.

High Point,[1] a coal mining community with a population of about 1,400 people, is located "up the holler" in northern West Virginia. Cursed with problems common to coal mining camps, there is nothing distinctive about its miseries. Remote police, poor sanitation, rough roads, lack of recreational opportunities, prevalent drunkenness — these are characteristics on which High Point has no monopoly.

But the people decided that it was their business and that of the mining corporation to change conditions. They felt that they could best accomplish their purpose by working through a community council. A young minister influenced the local United Mine Workers Union to vote for the organization of the council. A large community meeting was called to set up the organization and consider the most pressing problems. A temporary council was put into operation, with three officers and representatives from the union, the PTA, the church, the women of the community, the Negro population, and one at large. This meant representation from all groups, as there were no other organizations in the community.

The work of the community council focused on four projects: roads, the coal company's store policy, recreation, and health. The better roads project was thwarted when both the coal company and the county disclaimed responsibility for maintenance of certain roads. But the council succeeded in getting the "terrible" roads scraped and responsibility placed for future maintenance. There is also hope that some of the roads will be "black topped."

The people's grievances against the store were that prices were too high, the credit system was bad, and the store would make no contribution to the Sunday school or community. It was claimed, for instance, that the store would permit a man to charge groceries until he "got in a hole." Then it would make it hard for him, especially if he was a family man. When his wife came in for flour the manager would not sell flour, but he would sell bread, on which he made more profit.

Through the community council's efforts the store manager was removed, for it was discovered that he was making a special personal profit above the already high prices asked by the company. Under the new manager a much better credit relationship was established. The people also learned to buy outside as a means of protesting local bad practices.

The council also took on several recreational projects such

as Fourth of July and Labor Day celebrations, and the sponsorship of a Boy Scout troop.

The problem of sewage and water supply was pressing. Conditions were bad. For example, the house next to the parsonage was completely surrounded by open sewers. The people, many of whom had recently purchased houses from the company, were asked to improve sanitation. They responded in an encouraging way. A few years ago only three or four houses had inside toilets; now there are "fifty to seventy-five."

When it was discovered that the privately-owned water system was not delivering safe water the council consulted the owner. When the matter was not corrected the man was brought before the council, an experience new to him. At first he "was mad" but when he cooled down the water supply was purified. The community council asked for a report every three days from both the owner and the county health officer — and got it.

This community council is not old; it has been established less than a year. But already it has tackled some real needs and has had a large measure of success. Its greatest contribution cannot be measured or seen. It has helped people to be masters of their own destinies. They have begun to escape the dominance and paternalism of the company. They have begun to escape their own lethargy, irresponsibility, carelessness, and helplessness. If things are not right they can do something about them. They are moving toward a cleaner, more beautiful, more wholesome, more spiritual community. They are on the way. They can slip back, but they need not. The destiny of the community is in their hands.

In all this the church is central. The church, only two years old, preaches and teaches the Word on Sunday. During the week it brings in the kingdom by helping the people to understand and practise the abundant life where they are.

THE COMMUNITY AND HOME MISSIONS

The home mission enterprise, which seeks to carry the message of Christ and to extend the outreach of the church in new and old places, is much affected by the idea of community.

Imagine a village with a population of 600 people at the center and 700 more in the surrounding area. There are five churches: Roman Catholic, Episcopal, Presbyterian, Methodist, and Congregational. If the people were equally divided among these churches, there would be 260 for each church. Obviously that is not enough members to support the kind of church that the people want. Each of the Protestant churches has petitioned its home mission board for funds with which to augment the pastor's salary. These funds have been forthcoming and four denominations are taking money given by devoted Christians to help support four weak churches in a single small community.

These churches present a problem that has given the mission boards serious concern. Is a mission board justified in making an appropriation of funds to a church in an over-churched community? That community is not dependent upon any one church for the gospel. If one failed there would be others to witness. Obviously, the mission appropriations cannot make all these churches strong forces. The churches will likely "forever" ask for the annual appropriations, becoming so dependent that they express a special claim on the denominations' missionary funds. Would it not be best to get the churches together, help them take on greater force and become self-supporting, thereby releasing the mission grants for much needed work in other communities? Or, the mission money could be used to support an enlarged ministry in a united Protestant church!

Consider another situation faced by the mission boards. A new community is being born at the site of a huge government

dam. Five thousand persons are living in the area and before
the peak of construction is reached there will be twice that
number. After the dam is completed the permanent popula
tion will settle to about 2,500.

Obviously such a community needs the ministry of the
church. Many of the people are temporary residents seeking
economic reward more than the security of home and community. Many have little religious interest and there is not much
local impetus to build a church. Experience proves that almost
invariably outside aid is needed in getting established the kind
of church that people need.

Immediately the question arises as to how many churches
the community needs. About a dozen denominations are represented in this population in considerable number. Should each
of the twelve mission boards enter the community? Should
sufficient funds be appropriated to erect twelve church edifices
and twelve parsonages and to support twelve ministers? Or
should the church boards through the local council of churches
and through the Home Missions Council of North America
cooperate in providing one strong Protestant church for this
community?

The kind of answers that mission boards give to these questions will be determined in no small measure by the concept of
community. If a church is self-centered, it will give one answer;
if community-minded its answer will be — comity.

Comity is a plan devised for aiding communities to have one
church or only as many churches as the population warrants.
It was conceived and agreed upon by denominational administrators and church federation workers, locally and nationally.

There may be said to be three features of the plan for churching communities. There are allocation of fields to the denominations, withdrawal of aid from competing churches, and the
establishment of an interdenominational church.

Allocation works as follows: A survey is made of a new community, after which the denominational executives meet to consider churching it. After full consideration of the nature of the field, the state of readiness of the denominations, and other factors, the assignment is made to a denomination. Similarly other fields are assigned to other denominations. The community at the dam site might be dealt with in this way.

Withdrawal is the act by which one or more denominations agree to refrain from supporting churches in a community where competition exists. In the case of the community of 1,300 people and four Protestant churches three of the denominations might withdraw aid, thus encouraging the fourth to increase its effectiveness. *The Master List* is the technical name for the method used by five major denominations for eliminating competitive appropriations to churches in rural communities.[5]

Another expression of comity is the formation of an interdenominational or community church. Some churches so formed have been related to the Home Missions Council of North America, but in the course of time they become affiliated with some denomination as denominational community churches.

Comity has roots early in the settlement of the United States, when some effort was made to have one Protestant church for a given body of population. These beginnings are seen in the New England town church and in several types of union churches. But competition became the order of the day as the population moved westward. Peter Cartwright, the pioneer missionary, was zealous in preaching the gospel and almost as zealous in outdoing the "water baptizing Baptists." It is said that when the railways extended westward a missionary of one denomination could be seen riding the cowcatcher of the engine in order to arrive in town ahead of his less adventuresome competitor who rode the seats of the day coach. So the United States has been, in the large, churched competitively.

Farsighted leaders early saw the folly of this policy; they saw that too many churches in a community were as ineffective as too few. By 1913 the Home Missions Council had developed a comity statement. Several denominations agreed not to start new churches without consultation and to consider cases of complaints when it was felt that the action of one denomination in the local field was detrimental to another. Where circumstances justified, one denomination should retire from an over-churched field.

The present status of comity is expressed in a statement on comity principles for rural communities that forms a guide for the churching of rural communities.[6]

The Home Missions Council has recently reviewed the status of comity as applied to the whole church, urging the denominations to exert the utmost effort to clear the missionary slate of competitive projects.[7]

Comity in the future needs to be understood and practised more widely than ever before. Currently only a few of the many national boards practise it. On the state level the situation is even more serious. Before more boards will act by it they must see it as a positive, progressive, and necessary means of church strategy. Popularizing and interpreting the plan is essential to its wider acceptance.

Comity to be effective must be local. Local people must believe in it, must have a perfect understanding of the purpose behind it and the way in which it operates. It can never be effective so long as it is applied nationally by denominational boards without local support.

Local comity committees should be thoroughly grounded in the theory of cooperation to supplement the practice of withdrawal and allocation. It is easy for these committees to by-pass the practice of cooperation for a kind of superimposed administration by fiat.

There needs to be realism as to the maximum number of people that can be served by one church. In rural America there are usually too few people for a church. But occasionally comity committees do not provide for enough churches. Such an instance is seen in the deserts of eastern Washington, where a government housing project was assigned to one denomination, with other denominations agreeing to this arrangement. The population that grew rapidly increased to at least 15,000 before any effort was made to locate a second church. In the meantime certain non-cooperative groups had entered the community, partially vitiating the aims and efforts of the comity committee.

When the comity agreement was first put into effect, the signatory denominations were frequently the only ones concerned about the evangelization of a particular community. Not so today! For each area assigned to a particular denomination, there may be several other groups ready to enter without invitation. This situation complicates the operation of the comity plan. There seems to be no way to improve this condition except by a patient setting forth of the principles underlying comity.

It needs to be more widely recognized that comity was devised as a means of doing missionary work and the principles and practice of comity were born out of a missionary motive. Comity was a practice evolved on the missionary frontier. It was invented by men personally interested in missions. They conceived it as a means of systematizing and making effective the church outreach. Comity is therefore not meant to throttle or impede church work, but to make the work of the church more effective.

It needs to be remembered, too, that comity committees are

human. These committees make errors in judgment and they sometimes represent erroneous ideas. Comity committee members are made up of the same kind of stuff as are all other people. Errors have been made and will be made. But any such faults do not minimize the need for comity, which is still great. One national leader said, "The practice of comity sagged when the denominations received large postwar funds."

An illustration of comity is a story of two denominations that made surveys in a growing community. The area extended on both sides of a steep hill, with sizeable populations on either side. Both denominations were prepared to launch a new work and erect church buildings competitively. At that juncture it was suggested that one denomination choose one side of the hill and the other take the opposite slope. The counsel was followed with good results.

A Western parish is defined by a valley at least twenty by forty miles in extent. This field, allocated to one denomination, is served by a missionary, the only ordained Christian worker in the area. The population, made up of a few business people, miners, ranchers, sheepherders, and schoolteachers, stem from many denominations.

The pastor thinks it his duty to serve all and eventually to win all. Toward this end he arranges a regular Sunday service, two Sunday schools, young people's meetings, and Vacation Bible Schools. Church membership is open to all evangelical Christians. Quite typically, these services do not reach all the people, so he calls extensively, also visiting the three schools. He sometimes goes on horseback, and rides with others as well as driving his own car. But even by these means some are unreached. To multiply his contacts with some and to reach all, he prints a monthly bulletin. Through a short story, a sermonette, and announcements he brings a message to the people. By distribution through the local post office this paper eventually reaches the last sheepherder far back and up in his mountain watch.

Home missions may be described as an effort to serve people and include them in Christian fellowship. It may be said that there are two phases of home mission effort. First is the outreach of the local church into its immediate community, the "beginning in Jerusalem phase." Second is the "Judea and Samaria phase," which is the outreach of the church beyond the area of the church's immediate access or ability.

It is this second phase of home missions to which reference is usually made when the term "home missions" is used. The local church's role in this kind of missions is expressed through contributions of money made through denominational channels and mission boards. The contributions are used to support missionaries and institutions. The home mission enterprise carried on by Protestants is extensive and varied, with thousands of projects and full-time and part-time workers. It reaches the growing point of population; it is represented in areas of disintegration; and it is found in many places of special need or where the performance of a religious ministry is beset with particular difficulties.

The "beginning in Jerusalem phase" of home mission work often is not considered to be home mission work at all. Actually it can be the most fruitful phase. Millions remain unchurched in the United States who live within easy driving range of a church if not within the sound of a church bell. If these people are to be brought within the fellowship, it will be through the direct missionary outreach of the local church. Besides the driving imperative that constrains church people to win their near neighbors, there is the practical consideration that all the available funds given by the church will never be sufficient to support missionaries to perform this local missionary service.

It is precisely at this point that the community concept has made a large contribution to home missions by helping the local church to see that it is the center for the immediate and local mission thrust. The local church is the mission agency "in Jerusalem." The local church may arrange for the establishment of outpost Sunday schools, for church buses to transport children to services, for a religious news service to every home, for any plan or service necessary in the evangelization of its immediate area.

The home missionaries have been specialists in getting the church started. But, always, the methods used in establishing new churches were learned from the old. That is true today. All the methods, programs, points of view, and experiences of churches imbued with the spirit of the rural church movement need to be made available to the home mission growing edge. It is folly to use outmoded methods in home missions. It is difficult to imagine a place in rural America today where the points of view held by community-minded churches and pastors do not apply. The whole range of rural church interest needs to be applied to home mission work everywhere: among the Indians, the Mexicans, the bilingual churches, on the plains, in the mountains, on the growing outskirts of cities, in the South and in the North. A reformation in spirit and program would soon accompany a widespread introduction of such methods into the home mission enterprise.

References

1. "A Great Country Church," by Ralph A. Felton, in the *Progressive Farmer*, February, 1949. Used by permission.
2. A group of rural pastors classified the agencies operating in their communities into 10 groups as follows: agricultural, educational, health, the press, youth, business and professional, trade, patriotic, parks and grounds, lodges.

3. An article by Harold C. Kaufman, in *Town and Country Church*, May, 1949, p. 1.
4. The name is fictitious, the community real.
5. By 1935 the comity principle had become so much a part of the thinking of national church administratives that five boards, i.e. Methodist, Episcopal, Northern Baptist, Congregational Christian, Reformed in the U. S., and Presbyterian, U. S. A., joined in signing a master list agreement. (Eight or nine boards now participate in the Master List.) Through this Master List a list of missionary appropriations by each board for each state is kept. In instances where it is found that competing appropriations are being made, the national boards notify the regional conference or state ecclesiastical officers that national appropriations will be discontinued. The Executive Secretary of the Home Missions Council of North America was requested to follow up cases of competitive appropriations.
6. For a copy of this statement, write to: Committee on Town and Country, Home Missions Council, 297 Fourth Avenue, New York 10, N. Y.
7. Specifically, an effort was made to (1) think of comity in positive terms, a better churching of America; (2) gather more facts in order to make intelligent decisions; (3) make a further revision of the comity principles; (4) encourage mission boards to review current programs in the light of comity; (5) review the Master List and make an attempt to secure the acceptance of comity agreement by more mission boards; (6) bring the Master List up to date; and (7) have mission boards record their approval of accepted forms of comity cooperation.

CHAPTER 6

Join Hands Then

Julian, California, settled by the gold rushers, is now a quiet little village in the Sierra Mountains about fifty miles east of San Diego. The population of about 450 make a living from lumbering, apple orchards, vineyards, tourists, and summer camps.

Julian is the center of about one thousand square miles in which there are a number of small neighborhoods, among them Pine Hills, Ranchita, Witch Creek, and Mesa Grande. The total population in the entire area is not over twelve or fourteen hundred people.

There is a small Protestant church in Julian. It has seen some hard years. Since Julian is cut off from the cities and more populous rural districts by mountains, it has often had difficulty in securing pastors. Even now the membership of the church is only about forty and attendance at Sunday services averages from forty to fifty.

Yet, this may be called "the little church with the big outreach." The pastor considers the district of one thousand miles his parish and believes that the church should serve the people by the most effective means.

Knowing that people will not drive long distances to the central church, neighborhood meetings have been arranged at several points. Twenty to forty persons may attend the sessions, which combine devotion, instruction, and fellowship.

A home department mails pamphlets and communications to all families.

The pastor makes a practice of cooperating with the constructive community agencies. He keeps in close touch with the centralized school and is chaplain of the Grange. He is a member of the Chamber of Commerce and the Masonic Lodge and whenever possible works with the Foresters, the American Legion, the Auxiliary, Woman's Club, and the Kiwanis Club.

In calling, the pastor wears out his car, but he keeps in touch with people by visiting those at a distance as well as those at the center.

In order to provide a church home for all of evangelical persuasion, the church has provided for associate membership. It is seeking, though belonging to a single denomination, to be the spiritual home of all in the community.

Many churches, like the one in Julian, have learned that there are extensive resources available for the building of the community in county, state, regional, and national organizations. These agencies and resources have been made available out of concern for the rural situation. The wide-awake rural church, concerned for its community, will share resources of leadership, survey experience, technical skills, and inspiration.

FARMERS' ORGANIZATIONS

Farmers have long had their associations and organizations. Currently the Grange, the Farmers' Union, and the Farm Bureau Federation are the Big Three. They are exponents of a square deal for agriculture and rural life.

The *Patrons of Husbandry* (*the Grange*) is the oldest of the farm organizations, having had its origin in 1867. Its membership includes farmers and others interested in rural life in thirty-eight states. Its purpose has been summarized, "to educate and elevate the American farmer." Its chief functions are fraternal and educational. At first it sponsored extensive co-operative enterprises, but at present its economic efforts are confined to the field of insurance. It is the largest secret order in the world and its ritual and program emphasize the appreciation of rural values. It is strongly interested in legislation and maintains a Washington office.

The *Farmers' Union* was organized in the early 1900's as the Farmers' Education and Cooperative Union of America. It is composed of working farmers and their families. The central unit is the local organization. There is also a state organization in thirty-eight states and a national union. It is strongest in the Middle West.

Two of its principal emphases are the family farm as fundamental in rural life and in all society and democratic discussion and action. It operates more successful local farm cooperatives than any other farm organization in America. The strong interest of the Farmers' Union in education is channeled through a national director of education and through state staffs. Large support for this phase of the work comes through the local cooperatives.

The first *Farm Bureau* was organized in Broome County, New York, in 1911. From the first the Farm Bureau Federation has been organized on a county basis, not locally, as have been the other two farm organizations. It works closely with the county and state agricultural extension services. Along with other groups it encourages the 4-H clubs. Its national office is located in Chicago and it maintains legislative offices in Washington. The membership in December, 1948, embraced 1,325,-826 farm families, an increase of over 50,000 over the previous year.

The activities of the national Farm Bureau are so extensive as to require a staff of 57 employed officers, 42 in Chicago and 15 in Washington.

Two significant organizations of rural women are the *Associated Women of the American Farm Bureau Federation* and the *Associated Women of the World*. The former has an annual meeting with representatives from all the states. The 1948 convention program depicted a sailing vessel with seven sails titled recreation, education, rural youth, health, world peace, freedom, and religion. Religion on the top sail flew above all the others. That is somewhat symbolic of the emphasis in this organization.

The cooperative movement that seeks to "build men among men" is a growing force in rural life. The status of *cooperatives* among farmers can be described no better than it was by Harold Hedges, chief of the Cooperative Research and Service Division of the Farm Credit Administration:

Cooperation is a tradition in American agriculture. In pioneer days neighbors cooperated to build houses and barns, break new land, and harvest their crops. It was an easy step to the cooperative marketing of butter and cheese and the joint shipment and sale of livestock. Organized cooperative effort by American farmers is almost 140 years old. Early cooperatives were small organizations set up and operated by farmers in a single community and performing the local services of assembling, grading, packing, and shipping farm products.

Over the years cooperatives have expanded their services to include the marketing of farm products beyond the local shipping point and the manufacture and wholesaling of essential farm supplies. A substantial part of practically all farm products produced in commercial quantities are now handled at one or more stages in the marketing process by cooperative associations. In addition, cooperatives distribute feed, fertilizer, petroleum products, seed, farm machinery, and other supplies to the value of approximately $1,000,000,000.

The total dollar volume of 10,150 marketing and purchasing cooperatives was $6,070,000,000 for the marketing season 1945–46. Cooperatives offering services that are allied to marketing and purchasing include those operating cold-storage and frozen-food locker plants, public markets, storage and warehousing facilities, and associations engaged in transportation.

Farmers also have organized cooperatives to perform other types of service. Mutual fire insurance companies, irrigation associations, and mutual telephone companies have been in existence for many years. It is estimated that there are now 2,000 mutual insurance companies, 4,000 irrigation associations, 2,000 mutual telephone companies operating switchboards, and 30,000 rural telephone associations which do not operate switchboards. . . .

It is estimated that at least 6 out of every 10 farmers in the United States are members of one or more cooperatives engaged in marketing, purchasing, insurance, or other business services.

The success and stability of farmer cooperatives is due in large degree to the principles on which they have been established. It is a principle of cooperation that investment should be in proportion to use, that returns on capital should be limited, that cooperatives should be controlled by their members on a democratic basis, and that savings should be distributed to patrons in proportion to their patronage.[1]

The *weekly newspaper* is one of the phenomena of American rural life. Almost every town has one. The subscription list for many may be little more than a thousand, but the total number of subscribers runs into millions.

These papers carry principally local news, some quite gossipy and trite. Most of the papers are not exciting except to the local people who are concerned. Yet, by and large, they report faithfully the happenings in these communities.

There are *magazines* for rural people. Some of the largest, like the *Progressive Farmer* and the *Farm Journal*, have a circulation of several million.

No study has been made to gauge the difference between the rural papers and the urban and general publications. Some differences are quite evident. The urban newspapers have a higher quality of workmanship mechanically and editorially.

The rural magazines and papers represent a higher standard of living and of ethics. They do not play up the sensational. Liquor, beer, and wine advertisements are at a minimum in rural papers, while in the urban these things are portrayed in brilliant colors. The rural papers are prone to simplicity, while the urban tend toward sophistication.

All in all, the rural papers represent a high standard of excellence for rural communities and are instruments useful for the advancement of the good life in the countryside.

OTHER RURAL AGENCIES

A few of the numerous secular rural agencies should be examined.

The *United States Department of Agriculture* was established in 1862 for the purpose of serving the people of the nation, particularly the farmers. It is charged with acquiring and diffusing agricultural information. It is now a tremendous governmental department housed in a spacious building.

The United States Department of Agriculture has five principal functions, namely: (1) research, (2) education and program, (3) administration of Federal laws on the marketing and distribution of agricultural products, (4) the regulation of interstate commerce on food, fiber, and related products, and (5) protection and management of national forests, farm credit, agricultural adjustment, conservation, land use, farm rural rehabilitation, rural electrification, and other phases of agricultural interest.

It operates through bureaus such as the Bureau of Animal Husbandry. The Bureau of Agricultural Economics, the primary agency for gathering and disseminating agricultural statistics, is probably the best known.

The ramifications of the department are so many and intricate as to be almost inconceivable without a careful study. The facilities of a 500,000 volume agricultural library, the hundreds of bulletins, the services of the bureaus, offices, branches, and administrations, as well as the Extension Service — these all are available to the people who desire it. A few facts about several administrations and agencies will serve to illustrate the type of service offered.

The *Farmer's Home Administration*, established in 1946, is a worthy child of the depression-born Farm Security Administration. This agency works with the small farmer, often with those who cannot receive aid through the usual credit channels, sometimes with those who might be considered bad risks by the accepted standards of financing. It provides credit to improve farming operations or to aid farmers in becoming owners. Whenever desirable, it supplements its loans with individual guidance in farm and home management. Its record, like that of its predecessor, the Farm Security Administration, has won it favorable support from socially minded church people and others.

The *Farm Credit Administration*, organized in 1933 to combat the ruinous and distressful situation that confronted farmers, met such a need that it has been continued through the years of prosperity. Operating through 12 districts, this administration serves farmers in every section of the nation.

The *Rural Electrification Administration* has brought to the rural home light, heat, and power that have relieved drudgery, multiplied productive power, and brought comfort and delight. Established in 1935, it provided that farmers might organize large cooperative enterprises to manufacture or to purchase electric energy and distribute it to members. The record of success has been amazing. The consumption of energy has steadily increased with the ability to purchase new equipment and the discovery of additional uses.

The *state colleges of agriculture*, considering their scope and interests, might appropriately be called universities of agriculture. These land-grant colleges, one in each state, offer vast resources to rural people. Three divisions of labor are represented in each college: resident instruction, the experiment stations, and the extension service. Resident instruction is carried on by the resident faculty for the students. A director and a staff of technically qualified researchers man the research division. The extension service has a staff consisting of the director, supervisors, subject matter specialists, and agents in each county of the state. These county agents represent jointly the United States Department of Agriculture and the state college of agriculture. Through this agency the resources of the other two branches of the college become available to the most remote sections of the state.

The *Extension Service*, created in 1914, is an arm of the Department of Agriculture that disseminates useful and practical information among rural people. It operates chiefly in the broad field of agriculture and in home economics.

To the rural dweller the Extension Service is known through the county program, the nature of which is determined by the county planning committee and the agencies and interests with which it works. It embraces all the forces at work in the field of agriculture and home economics.[2] Serving in the counties are county agricultural agents, county club agents, and home demonstration leaders. The office of the agent is usually located in the county seat, and the program is sponsored by the county board of supervisors.

The *4-H Club* is probably the most widely known of all rural youth organizations. It is a part of the national Extension Service with headquarters in Washington and with state offices in the colleges of agriculture. It operates on a county basis with a county 4-H leader directing the program. The local 4-H Club is organized on a neighborhood basis.

The aim of the 4-H Club is to foster an all-round development of the boy and girl through teaching improved methods of agriculture and home economics and the finer things of rural life. The development of leadership is given particular stress.[3]

There are many activities carried on by these clubs, including conducted tours in summer to visit the projects of the members. Clubs quite commonly cooperate with the churches in observing Rural Life Sunday, the seed-time service.

The *Future Farmers of America* is an organization of high school students who are taking vocational agriculture. The vocational agriculture teacher offers courses of a practical nature in agriculture, shop, and related subjects. He also counsels and supervises the work of the students on their farms. The teacher is commonly employed on a year-round basis with the summer months devoted to supervision. Sometimes the school shops are opened to adults in the community.[4]

Among the other well known rural youth organizations are the *Juvenile Grange* and the *Junior Farmers' Union*. The Juvenile Grange is sponsored by the local Grange for children under 14 years of age. Through these units the youth are indoctrinated with the philosophy of rural life and are given leadership training and experience. Likewise, the Farmers' Union sponsors the Junior Farmers' Union, of which it has been said, "It is recognized everywhere as one of the most hopeful and dynamic rural social forces."

The agricultural agencies have accumulated a body of information and experience about the rural community that is invaluable. Innumerable studies of rural communities, special phases of community interest, and of churches have been made. This material is available to the rural church. Heeding some of it would help to avoid many a calamity in rural enterprises. It would give ideas and directions that would help programs to walk instead of stumble along.

If a community is interested in a community council, it does not need to search far to get in touch with materials and with someone who has had wide experience in the field. The same is true in health, recreation, home management, agriculture practices, and cooperative organizations.

RURAL CHURCH AGENCIES

Rural church forces have organized agencies and instituted services more specifically related to the church enterprise. The most obvious and spectacular evidence of the church's organized rural interest is the annual Convocation on the Church in Town and Country, a national interdenominational gathering for those interested in the rural church. Attendance runs to the thousand mark, with special services bringing in many more. Ministers predominate, but laymen, sociologists, specialists in religious education, economists, and many others are present. Some eighteen seminars meet in conjunction with the convocation.

Manifestations of the church's organized rural concern are seen in emphases upon rural values within the worship of local congregations. A sizeable collection of quality hymns for use on special rural life occasions has been introduced.[5] Interest has been revived in the observance of Rogation Sunday under the new name Rural Life Sunday. Each year since 1929 an order of service has been prepared for use in the church. Churches and farm organizations make wide use of it. In 1942, for the first time, a service for observance of Harvest Festival was prepared and published. This service has been continued since that time.

The *Committee on Town and Country* is the organization through which the cooperating denominations carry on these and other elements of their rural life program. It is a group of over one hundred denominational representatives who bring together the rural planning of their boards, the Home Missions Council, the Federal Council of Churches, and the International Council of Religious Education.

Since 1912, the Committee on Town and Country has cooperated with state colleges of agriculture and others in encouraging and providing leadership for in-service training schools for ministers. Twenty-five such schools and conferences were announced for the year 1949. Many more denominational schools and scores of conferences were held, many of which had their start from the example set by the interdenominational schools.

The committee publishes a magazine for the rural minister under the title *Town and Country Church*. From a very modest beginning it has enjoyed a steadily growing circulation and influence. Its 16 pages appearing nine times a year are bringing a lively response. It carries a wide variety of materials about rural church methods, programs, helps, outlook, and experiences. An aim of this magazine is to encourage church cooperation in rural communities.

The committee from time to time issues a statement on some phase of rural life. One statement, *Man and Land*, was signed by Protestants, Catholics, and Jews. It contained general expressions of principle relative to man's relationship to land. It received wide acceptance by people of many different viewpoints.

From these various statements it is possible to ascertain the thinking of American Protestants relative to certain phases of rural church advance.

In a real sense all efforts of the Committee on Town and Country are bent toward the serving of the local churches in the interest of winning the people individually and the communities as a whole to fullness of life in Christ.

Departments of town and country work are now an essential

part of most major denominations. Following the early example of the Presbyterian, Congregational, and Methodist boards of home missions, at least twelve denominations have added to their national staffs a director of rural church work. A number of these directors carry responsibility for the administration of mission funds. Several confine their efforts to a more specialized field of service to rural churches.

The Evangelical United Brethren Church's statement of the purpose of its rural department gives insight into the work of all. It is to "keep uppermost the spiritual meaning of life, in relation to rural living, the land, the home, the community, the church, Christ and God; striving by an inclusive, long-term strategy, based on thorough study and sound planning, to bring into existence the abundant life in Jesus Christ for all who are a part of the rural communities, through strengthening the ministry and influence of the rural parishes." [6]

Other denominations define the task in terms of developing a more effective ministry and program, promoting conferences, schools, and in-service training, developing literature, and upholding Christian concepts of agriculture.

Scores of district, synodical, state, and area specialists can be added to the list of rural leaders. They stimulate by every means possible the development of the churches along the line of progressive rural church work.

The *Christian Rural Fellowship*, with headquarters in New York, is a nondenominational body that promotes an understanding and appreciation of the religious and spiritual values that abide in the processes and relationships of agriculture and rural life. Its bulletin appears in the form of "papers" that are circulated to a world-wide membership. There are a number of state branches. The Christian Rural Fellowship occasionally publishes a "tested" rural church book or pamphlet.

Agricultural Missions, Incorporated is closely allied with the

Christian Rural Fellowship. It serves the cause of rural missions abroad and arranges for special training for foreign missionaries on furlough. The organization publishes *Rural Missions*, "a journal devoted to the development of Christian agriculture and rural life around the world." It is helpful to churches in the United States, as well as to those in other parts of the world. Another publication of the Agricultural Missions, Incorporated is the *Rural Church at Worship*.

The *Rural Church Institute* is an example of an interdenominational agency giving special service to the rural church. The headquarters are located at the student religious center on the campus of Cornell University, Ithaca, New York. It is entirely separate from the university, but it cooperates closely with the College of Agriculture. A primary idea in the minds of its founders was to establish for the churches of New York State an extension service comparable to that carried on for rural people by the College of Agriculture. It has been doing exactly that since its organization in 1935.

The Rural Church Institute is organized as a separate entity but it serves also as the rural department of the interdenominational state council of churches. Its support comes from the denominations as well as from interdenominational sources and from direct gifts.

Its program on the university campus includes cooperation with the College of Agriculture in planning an annual Rural Church Day during Farm and Home Week, arranging for rural church radio programs, and planning meetings for students interested in the rural church. In the summertime there is a school for ministers, a school of dramatics and another for lay leaders. There is also close cooperation with the school for missionaries held in the wintertime.

The field program has many phases. One emphasis maintained consistently is to help the churches of a community see their common task and to work together in accomplishing it. The institute has made surveys, helped local churches federate, organized larger parishes and groupings, and has assisted churches in extending their outreach. The fact that there are about ninety federated churches in New York, the largest number claimed by any state, is somewhat due to the efforts of the Rural Church Institute. The institute is a rallying point for people concerned that the churches unite the rural community for Christ.

A movement somewhat comparable is under way in Ohio, where rural life leaders and rural churchmen are spearheading a movement for a community-serving rural church.

Anyone in search of *literature* on the rural church can find it in abundance. This material may be grouped into four types. First are the magazine articles. There are scores of such articles each year in farm magazines and religious periodicals. Rural church columns are printed in some of our weekly papers as well as in religious periodicals.

Second are the pamphlets and booklets, of which the number is legion. Principal publishers are the state colleges of agriculture, denominational departments of town and country work, the Committee on Town and Country, and other agencies in the field related to rural work.

Third are the organs and periodicals published by denominational fellowships, seminaries, state departments of town and country work, national societies, interdenominational agencies, and others.

Fourth are the books. A few of real merit have been coming from the press. Valuable in addition to the current books are the old ones of classic value that have been rediscovered in our day. Gradually a rural church library is being built up.

While the *Roman Catholic rural life agencies* do not directly serve Protestant churches, the rather phenomenal rise of the

Roman Catholic rural interest and program has startled many
Protestants.

The Roman Catholics at a considerably later day than the
Protestants awoke to the critical situation relative to rural
Christianity. But once awakened, they developed a rural program with astonishing rapidity. The national Catholic Rural
Life Conference with headquarters in Des Moines, Iowa, is the
agency that spearheads the program. The executive secretary,
Monsignor Luigi G. Ligutti — dynamic, able, and versatile —
is the central figure. There is an annual conference, a publication, *The Christian Farmer*, and schools and conferences for
priests and others. Several authoritative books and a manual
for the clergy describing rural agencies and resources have been
published. *A Manifesto on Rural Life* states their views on rural
matters.

They are laying great emphasis upon the family farm, settling
families on the land, placing Displaced Persons, extending the
Roman Catholic Church in rural districts, and providing a
program of spiritual nurture to rural communicants.

The Roman Catholic Church recognizes that the city
churches depend upon a supply of rural people to maintain
themselves, that rural America is chiefly of Protestant background and preference, that Protestant rural churches are not
too effective in reaching the people. Monsignor Ligutti with
a twinkling but serious eye challenges Protestant audiences,
"We would rather see rural America Protestant than pagan. If
it is going to be pagan, we are going out there. We invite you
to go along, but we are going whether you go or not."

The contribution of Roman Catholic efforts to Protestants
is in the soundness of certain ideas advanced and in awakening
Protestants to the potentialities of the rural fields.

The *Jewish Agricultural Society*, which operates with the support of endowment funds, seeks to "encourage and advance

farming by Jews in the United States." Within the decade ending in 1947, 10,000 persons sought its advice, and 1,136 families were settled through its direct aid and many more indirectly. It also places workers on farms and aids in other rural programs of improvement.

These resources of materials, facilities, and leadership are extensive beyond the knowledge of most people, yet quite available to the local rural church. For instance, in West Virginia church leaders sensed a great unmet need in the coal mining communities. It was soon recognized that an intelligent and aggressive program was dependent upon fuller knowledge of the situation. When a study was launched in 1948, those participating were the state denominational bodies, the state council of churches, a committee of the Federal Council of Churches of Christ in America, and national departments of town and country work. Without the help of these larger agencies the task would have been far more difficult.

The outside leaders available for the local community are a means of giving inspiration and morale to local leaders. A minister, after attending a conference in which a number of national leaders participated, said that these men opened to him the field of rural service through the rural church, and he no longer felt alone, or like Don Quixote tilting at windmills. Perhaps this represents one of the great needs among rural leaders; there is a feeling of standing alone, a sense of futility through lack of recognition. When rural leaders pause to think of the talent and facilities available to them they can feel a part of a great and growing company.

References

1. *Bibliography on Cooperation in Agriculture*, Introduction. United States Department of Agriculture Library Literary List No. 41, Washington, D. C., June, 1948. Used by permission.

2. The service usually embraces 15 principal interests: (1) livestock, (2) dairy, (3) poultry, (4) veterinary, (5) agronomy, (6) horticulture, (7) entomology, (8) plant pathology, (9) soil conservation, (10) agricultural engineering, (11) economics, (12) home management, (13) clothing, (14) nutrition, and (15) parent education and child development.

3. Much is made of the fourfold purpose expressed symbolically in the four-leaf clover emblem and verbally in the pledge: "I pledge: my *head* to clearer thinking, my *heart* to greater loyalty, my *hands* for larger service, and my *health* to better living, for my club, my community, and my country." The training for 4-H Club members includes practical training in various agricultural and home economics practices, the carrying on of supervised projects in these fields, training in the conduct of meetings, leadership, judging, and public speaking, and the development of self-reliance, ambition, and initiative. Membership is open to boys and girls between the ages of 10 and 21 years. Local clubs meet twice a month under the direction of leaders selected and trained by the county 4-H leader.

4. The purposes of the F.F.A., as the name is commonly abbreviated, are:
   To develop competent, aggressive rural and agricultural leadership;
   To create and nurture a love of country life;
   To strengthen the confidence of farm boys and young men in themselves and their work;
   To create more interest in the intelligent choice of farming occupations;
   To encourage members in the development of individual farming programs and establishment in farming;
   To encourage members to improve the farm home and its surroundings;
   To participate in worthy undertakings for the improvement of agriculture;
   To develop character, train for useful citizenship, and foster patriotism;
   To participate in cooperative effort;
   To encourage the practice of thrift;
   To encourage improvement in scholarship;
   To provide and encourage the development of organized rural recreational activities. — *Agricultural Handbook for Rural Pastors and Laymen,* by Thomas E. Howard, pp. 109–110. National Catholic Rural Life Conference, 1946. Used by permission.

5. *Hymns of the Rural Spirit.* New York, Federal Council of the Churches of Christ in America, 1947.

6. Informal Report, 1948.

CHAPTER 7

Christian Dynamics for Community Living

The Christian community is an elusive ideal. For that reason it is held by some to be impractical. "But is there and can there be such a thing as a Christian community?" the query goes, as if to say through interrogation that there can be no such thing, so why bend efforts in that direction.

In a sense, the making of a Christian community may be compared to the art of painting. Great artists perceive reality. Then they seek to represent it through color, form, balance, and perspective. Physical representations are used to convey a notion of the timeless and eternal. Through the particular the artist reveals the universal and through the passing and transitory that which is permanent.

All great artists press toward perfection; none achieve it, but some approach it. It has been said that Michelangelo was "a man of tempestuous moods and godlike yearnings who sought to achieve the impossible and came as near to it as any mortal man." [1] Any less effort to see abiding truth and to portray it would not have made his paintings immortal.

The perception of the Christian community comes only to those of discerning mind and of good heart. The actual communities that men create are representations of the ideal. There are communities that approach the ideal because people of good will pursue it with more than ordinary deftness and zeal.

The development of the Christian community does not await the elimination of all sin and shortcomings any more than peace between nations awaits the perfection of all persons within the nations. The foundation of the community rests solidly on the character of good people. In Christian communities good will does not eliminate tension and discord but it always transcends them. Cooperation outruns competition, the valuation placed on the nonmaterial keeps in balance the emphasis on the material.

A Christian community is inspired by heaven and it is God-directed, but still it is made out of the stuff of the earth. Its achievement cannot await the sublimation of man into an ethereal sainthood. It begins now with men of earth who see visions of the new community on earth, a colony of heaven in a specific locality, and with men who have capacities to lead into the achievement of this community. Though men and communities may be made of clay, they are made to live by the breath of God.

"Ye therefore shall be perfect, as your heavenly Father is perfect" is a direction not only for individuals but for communities. To stop moving in that direction is as fatal to the community as to the individual. To press toward the mark is as fruitful for the many as for the one.

DYNAMIC FOR BUILDING THE
CHRISTIAN COMMUNITY

Is the building of the Christian community as much an imperative as is the commission of Jesus to preach the gospel in all the world? Jesus' teachings supply ample motive for community building, particularly his teachings on human relationships and unity.

Throughout his ministry Jesus referred to God as his Father and the Father of men. In the same manner he referred to men as brothers. When Jesus prayed "Our Father" he sketched the lines of a family portrait: one household, the family of God and men. There are no secret words, rituals, or creeds required for membership in this family. The elementary fact that one is born and alive is sufficient warrant for each person to become a member. No one person, group, or class can exclude anyone else from this family. The privilege of belonging can be accepted or refused only by the person for himself. Every man has a standing invitation to share in the family of God and men. There is no exclusiveness about it.

Furthermore, there is throughout Jesus' ministry a strong emphasis upon making the family-of-God relationship effective in community living. The Good Samaritan was praised for helping the man he found in need. When Jesus was in Samaria he expressed the same magnanimity and interest in the "natives" as he did in a Judean or Galilean. The fact of physical or geographic proximity was one of the strongest factors in determining the application in Jesus' teachings. His gospel was a gospel for all the world, but all the world began right where he lived.

To argue from this that Jesus had a modern conception of the community requires a rather long leap of the imagination. Yet, it can be concluded without violation of the spirit of Jesus that his conception of the family of men in God and his concern for those with whom he had face-to-face contacts make the gospel applicable to the community in a special way. People within a comprehensible, local area can uniquely demonstrate that they belong to the family of God. God's love becomes more real as it is expressed to brothers whom one sees and sees frequently rather than to brothers whom one does not see at all or infrequently.

Jesus' teachings on unity are just as prominent as the teachings about the Fatherhood of God. When Jesus said "I am the vine; ye are the branches" he was not only describing the relationship between himself and the disciples but also between the disciples. The disciples were not the branch but branches, growing from one trunk. The trunk was a unifying center toward which the branches focused. So Christ is the center of the fellowship of unity of Christian people. It is recorded that Jesus prayed ardently for unity of the disciples with one another as well as with God.

These teachings of Jesus made a strong impression upon Paul. He says that God has made all men of one blood; that nationality and race are as nothing compared to the oneness of men. To those who adhered to factions in the Corinthian church he says that Christ has not been divided. At another point Paul compares the body of Christ, the church, to the human body. The body is made up of many diverse parts, some of lesser and some of greater importance and each part with a special form and function. These diverse parts making one unified body exemplify the principle of unity and togetherness that characterizes the true church of Jesus Christ.

While Christians throughout the centuries often neglected these teachings of Jesus and Paul, they have recurrently come to the forefront. Now they are being applied to the community. What, then, are the implications of these teachings for the community?

It is very apparent that differences of theological interpretation, nationality, race, economic or social status, or cultural standards are not sufficient reason for schisms in a church or for the establishment of several competing churches. There is no New Testament sanction for establishing churches on the foundation of such differences. To do so is a distinct compromise with the ideal of unity.

Similarly, there is no sanction for the establishment of churches on ill will, personal animosities, grudges, insults and personal pride. The incentive for contributing one hundred dollars for every foot by which the Methodist church steeple tops the Baptist spire does not have its impetus from Jesus' teachings. All persons, being human, are prone to possess these sins to a degree and to have their actions sometimes dictated by them. But Christians should not be so blind to the nature of the church of Christ that they will be party to these sins.

Diversity of "graces and gifts," ability, inclination, temperament, and outlook may be the means of giving variety and strength that a church sorely needs. A church or the churches can never, never come to the spirit and the fact of unity if that unity is expected to grow out of uniformity. The church was never meant to be characterized by uniformity. Such a church would be uninteresting and dull. It would be about as sensible for the nurseryman to set out to make all the flowers in the world one variety of daffodils as to attempt to make church members conformable to one pattern. The church takes on life through the particular, unhampered, and God-inspired contribution of each person to it.

Yet, the church seeks such forms of organization, patterns of practice, and worship as will satisfy the temperaments and appreciations of the largest number of people. The utmost of freedom and expression is to be allowed within the framework of a church united in spirit and organization. Of course, the frame of reference is always Christ.

IDEALS THAT SUPPORT THE CHRISTIAN COMMUNITY

Certain ideas and ideals, currently the focus of considerable interest, are dynamic aids in Christianizing the community. Such ideals, like a rising tide, can help lift the loads the church is trying to carry. The church always yields its best fruitage when its own ideals are supported by ground-swells of concern and interest in the community. Two of the most potent current ideals are the family farm and the productive home.

THE FAMILY FARM AND PRODUCTIVE HOME IDEALS

The growing interest in the *family farm* arises out of the discovery that the way land is held and used is a strong factor in determining the quality of life, for individual, family, community, and even the nation and the world. If, for instance, the family farms in Lancaster County, Pennsylvania, were broken up, most of the buildings taken down or made into apartments or barracks for workers, and the land operated in blocks of ten thousand acres, obviously a new type of rural life would emerge. The workers likely would have little security and would take on the personal qualities produced by insecurity. The income of the land would be less evenly distributed, so the local institutions would be supported paternalistically by a few large givers, or they would be poorly supported. Several well known factors would work against widespread participation in local community affairs. Standards of living and standards of life would sink. The community would be less democratic, less self-reliant, and less capable of developing persons of stature.

A study of two California communities, one with extensive land holdings and commercialized operation and the other with a maximum of family farms, gave evidence that the family type of community enjoyed more benefits of a social, educational, civic, cultural, economic, and religious nature. This, then, demonstrates the evident truth that there are superior forms of land tenure. The Family Farm is the form that contributes most to the development of the individual and all his relationships and responsibilities.

This ideal envisages a farm on which a family lives and by using all its skills and talents earns enough to provide adequately for clothing, diet, housing, health, education for all members, recreational, social, and religious opportunities, and security for old age. It emphasizes farming as a way of life quite as much as it does the economic aspects. It has been pointed out that:

Wherever land tenure has been discussed in Protestant gatherings, the conclusion is that the owner-operated, family-type farm in American agriculture is a goal to be desired and sought. The two basic considerations most frequently pointed out are: (1) that this type of agriculture is most conducive to fundamental human values and hence the church has a moral concern for its perpetuation; and (2) that this type of agriculture is most conducive to community stability and hence the church has a self-interest in its perpetuation.[2]

There is a wide chasm between the ideal of the family farm and the realization of it. The trend is toward bigger farms on one hand and the subsistence farm on the opposite extreme.

This trend makes the ideal of a family farm seem rather impractical. It does face some serious obstacles. Among these are increasing mechanization with emphasis upon big machinery and efficiency, the cost of buying and equipping a farm, the difficulties of financing, the vagaries of the economic cycle, the problems of transferring farm from father to son, unsatisfactory partnership arrangements, land inadequate as to extent and fertility, and the failure to possess an adequate ideal of rural living.

Yet the ideal persists as the highest conception of life for persons and families. This is the goal toward which the clearest thinkers on the potentialities of rural and national life are aiming.

The corporation farm has been named as a type antithetical to best rural interests. A corporation farm is usually a large holding, often operated by managers or by the owner as a business enterprise, employing permanent hired hands or transients. It is characterized by large scale production, and, in certain types of farming such as fruit growing, by the employment of large numbers of persons seasonally. The workers usually have no ownership privileges, little security of tenure, and no sickness, accident, or old-age benefits. As a whole, housing facilities are poor and the participation in community activities, including the church, is low.

The *productive home* ideal promises much for the future of a family living on the land. The basic concept is that of a family receiving most of its income from nonfarm sources, located in a "productive home" on a small plot of land. Here, through cooperative effort, it will use spare time in producing for home consumption and in developing skills and crafts according to interest and need. It will enjoy the social, cultural, and spiritual benefits associated with life on the land. The concept of a way of living is quite as central to the productive home as are any specific practices. The practice of this way of life is old in American history. But it takes on fresh significance because of new factors and forces at work. There are, for instance, more people who can practise this way of life — people living in small towns and the commuters who can have one foot on the land in a productive homestead.

Shorter hours of work, the extension of electricity to rural areas, and the manufacture of midget tractors and numerous other labor-saving devices make such a life possible without back-breaking effort.

These homes will be characterized by gardens, flocks of fowls, even a goat or a cow, by the practice of home arts, the maintenance of property, and by developing such skills as handicrafts and painting. There is an emphasis upon family solidarity and cooperation and the nurture of wholesome family life. There is

INSECURE TENURE

NO COMMUNITY CONTACTS

SOIL DEPLETION

BAD LIVING CONDITIONS

SECURE TENURE

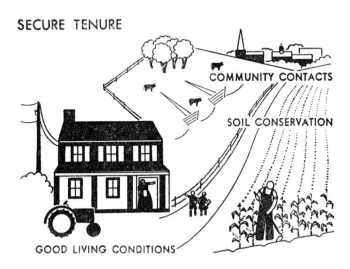

COMMUNITY CONTACTS

SOIL CONSERVATION

GOOD LIVING CONDITIONS

no fixed pattern, but a general emphasis upon a way of life geared to the land.

The Green Valley Church in Ohio turned to this idea as a means for a more effective community service. It wanted a pastor and couldn't get one. Some of the aggressive farmers called a meeting to find a way. The result was that a proposal was made to offer a comfortable home and a farm for the pastor they hoped to find.

Some agreements were arrived at. The farm was to be owned by a local corporation separate from the church but managed by some of the most active laymen in the church.

James D. Wyker writes of the vision that led to the purchase of the farm:

Perhaps you want to know just how Green Valley will utilize this farm: The answer will somewhat depend upon the wishes of the pastor and wife whom the church calls. The people expect the parson's family to get part of their livelihood from the soil. This will include not only a garden but some long-time subsistence production of such commodities as berries and fruit, milk, meat, honey, and eggs. The parsonage family will have all the acreage it can use for these agricultural arts. The balance of the land will be managed and operated by the farmers and the revenue therefrom will be turned over to the church.

This method of finance is known as the Lord's Acre Plan. What an opportunity this farm will be for demonstrating the answers to a dozen rural church needs! . . .

The people also agreed that Green Valley Church must be a community project in scope and spirit. This congregation has been moving in this direction for years but now the people have committed themselves to take their church pattern from, and build their program on, community needs. . . .

This democratic decision to make their church community-centered indicates that these farmers have some reasonable feelings which are not clearly defined, but nevertheless powerful. In my feeble way I will state some of these spiritual "hunches": The church must be as big as its community. Sectarianism must cease being divisive in families or communities. The churches that spiritualize agencies will also spiritualize their people.[3]

Green Valley is not alone in this approach. Many pastors weary of dividing efforts among scattered small churches, want to put their roots down in one community.

Some of the benefits of this mode of living are the enjoyment that the families receive from creative activities, a higher level of living, the additional security found in productive practices, the hedge against depression and old age, the appreciation of the nature and experience of the natural world, and identification with the people among whom one lives.

The importance of this way of life cannot be overestimated for millions of people. It can bring to nonfarm people the type of security and enjoyment that the family farm brings to the farmers. Fishermen, miners, lumbermen, professional people, factory workers, merchants, schoolteachers, and many others belong to the group to whom this way of life offers great advantages. It will encourage the subsistence farmer to "live" in his home instead of "subsist" in it.

This ideal, when fortified by Christian teachings and the goal "every home a Christlike home" is a great asset to the task of the church in Christianizing the community.

THE STEWARDSHIP OF LIFE

Another ideal strengthening the rural community is stewardship. Stewardship proclaims man's responsibility for the care and keeping of his body, his soul, the land and other natural resources, his time, and his talents. Everything belongs to God, and men are the recipients and users of God's bounty. All those resources by which a family and a community live the steward administers to the good of man and to the glory of God.

The Reverend Clyde Leeds, pastor of the Disciples Church, Garden City, Minnesota, provides a good example of one who led a church to new power through a well conceived program of stewardship.

Mr. Leeds first saw the church property in 1942. It was run down and unsightly. Something had to be done about it. It made a bad impression. Mr. Leeds might have organized a high pressure campaign to raise funds for the needed repairs. But he was interested in more than repairing the church and in making the parsonage attractive. He wanted the people of the church and community to develop in Christian character. He wanted the church to minister effectively to the community.

At a meeting of the elders, the Lord's Acre Plan was discussed. Some of them had heard about the plan over the radio. It was made a matter of prayer. Finally, the plan was brought before the large official board that represents most of the families in the church. A plan called "God's Portion" was approved and put into operation.

This plan is not operated as a scheme, but it is based upon sound Biblical principles. It follows the New Testament teaching of stewardship. It belongs to the Old Testament tradition of bringing the first fruits. The people who give to the God's Portion may substitute it for the regular giving if they desire. But the pledge card on one side provides for money gifts, on the other side for God's Portion gifts, a portion of the flock or field or the work of one's hands.

This is the way the God's Portion Plan works. The pledges are taken by the deacons at the time of the every member enlistment. The pastor believes in the New Testament teaching in which the minister takes leadership in preaching, teaching, and training. The officers and workers in the church extend the outreach of the church through its various organizational and physical ministries.

When people pledge through the God's Portion they can designate not only what they will dedicate but name the purpose for which the gift will be used. During 1948 some of the gifts were as follows: 1 hog, ½ acre corn, 4 hogs, 12 dozen eggs, an acre of peas, ½ acre of corn from a widow. A master carpenter donated the wages received on June 1, July 1, August 2, and September 1. The total was $66.50. This was in addition to his tithing. Fifty-seven persons gave God's Portion gifts.

An annual festival is held in the autumn. Sometimes this is in connection with a morning service. After a dinner, there is a service to receive the cash from the God's Portion gifts. The last God's Portion brought in $2,000.

The farmers in this community are quite prosperous. The pastor says, "I want the people to have the best for themselves, but I don't want them to be selfish. They should remember others."

The church also works on the theory that if people dedicate a portion of field or flock and care for it as dedicated it will do much toward rebuilding a religious attitude into the lives of the people.

Likewise, a church that is practising sound stewardship always has money on hand to do those things that need to be done. That does away with the need for drives and pay suppers and other schemes for wringing money from people.

The people give freely. No one is persuaded. The every member enlistment program is thorough, but it is used as a means of building the church.

Furthermore, much is made of the missions program of the church. The theory is that having compassion for those in need will open up the springs of giving for the local program.

The experience of the church since 1942 has demonstrated the wisdom of its course. Here are some of the records:

Resident membership has increased from 128 in 1942 to 156

in 1948. The current expense budget increased from $2,400 in 1942 to $5,901.57 in 1948. The number of tithers increased from 4 to 27. The amount raised for missions in 1928 was $3,562.24. The per capita giving in 1948 was $22.83, the highest of 46 churches of its denomination in the state. The Garden City church has pledged itself to raise over one-tenth of the total amount of money set as the state goal for a special world mission effort. Six hundred dollars was given to the Week of Compassion collection for Church World Service. The church contributes annually to the Child Saving Institute in Omaha, Nebraska. The collection for CROP amounted to over $500 in 1948.

This added giving has meant a great deal for the strengthening of the church's ministry in the community. The church building has undergone extensive repairs. The parsonage has been painted outside and inside; a modern bath and an oil burning furnace have been installed. The very appearance of the buildings gives the church a new place of service in the community.

A larger service is done through the pastor. His salary has climbed from $1,200 to $2,400 and parsonage. Recognizing that the minister is a community leader, an extra expense account of $87.50 per month is made to cover his travel and other church and community work. Besides this, the church provides for office expense in publishing the bulletin and for other services. This church is not scraping the bottom and cutting corners and crippling its outreach for lack of funds.

The church building is the center for many community meetings. It is available without cost for the regular meetings of the 4-H Club and the Boy Scouts. The Home Demonstration Council and other agricultural meetings are held in the church. All this and more is being done by a church supported by a hamlet of 350 people and the people in the adjacent countryside.

WHAT MUST THE CHURCH DO?

The ideal of the Christian community is of great importance to the local church. This significance has been clearly stated by Professor Maynard L. Cassady, in an address made shortly before his untimely death in 1948. He said that first the church must grow strong within itself, achieve keener spiritual insights and greater power. This is imperative. Secondly, the church must "release the leaven of the gospel into the intricate patterns of human relations in local community living."[4]

Relative to the second imperative the church has three specific functions:

First, the church regards all agencies, groups, organizations, institutions of the community as potential spiritual forces. It therefore works through them or with them, rather than creating a rival set of agencies or institutions. The church's method is that of persuasion, criticism, and conciliation, not that of control, direct or indirect. . . .

The second specific function of the church in the community is that it is to operate through the daily vocations of its members. This is an almost forgotten function today. To many, the church is always to be represented in the community by the pastor. He must sit on committees; attend functions; be an authority on housing, race relations, care for the aged, control of venereal disease, juvenile delinquency, and the real estate tax rate. The actual experts in these fields and others are those members of the church having special talents, skills, abilities, and occupational experience. What they need — which most Christian laymen today lack — is some understanding of the bearing which the gospel has upon the human relationships which operate every hour and day within their respective vocations and interest groups. The function of the church, therefore, under the skillful leadership of the pastor is the preparation and training of the laity for this task. The pastor would need to know his community thoroughly but not need to disperse his energies; instead he would concentrate them on the congregation. He would use the strategy of small groups, cells, individual action rather than seek approval for every move by the entire congregation; he would constantly call on the expert to aid him in this training. He would see the church, not as a specialist in community affairs, tinkering with this, repairing that; patching here, restoring there; rushing from one emergency to another — a session on public health today, a conference on the control of atomic energy tomorrow. He would see the church approach the community, integrally, as a whole, and become one of the means for preserving the unity and cohesion of community life.

The third specific function of the church . . . is to preserve the wholeness, the integrity of the community.[5]

In order to do this, Professor Cassady feels that it must comprehend the whole community.

More than any other institution, the church must "see life steadily and see it whole." The church looks at people rather than at problems; it deals with people as whole beings, not as fragments, not as "souls" divorced from the material secular bodies. This means that the church works primarily through the two institutions in which people are seen as wholes rather than parts: the family and the community itself. In the family and the community the fragments of individual living are most completely pieced together. In the school, the club life, the professional society, the union, the occupation, the lodge, the individual lives only part of his life. There may be no real coherent unity among these various groups to which he belongs. . . . This approach strikes directly at some of the sources of cultural disintegration: atomistic living, fear and insecurity, the hardening of class lines. It is the fact that the church is primarily concerned with people, not with things, that frees it for the task uniquely.[6]

Dr. Cassady sums up under five headings the implications to the church of the community idea:

First, a fundamental shift in strategy by the churches from a vertical to horizontal operation, *i.e.*, communitywise rather than denominationwise. Cultic differences should be accepted for what they are in true Protestant tradition — historical relativities, human preferences, not barriers to corporate fellowship in matters of conduct.

Second, a philosophy of community is seriously needed — a philosophy which correlates the work of social scientists with the teachings and insights of the Christian religion. Such would provide a common meeting ground and would also become the basis for a new strategy in Christian work. . . .

Third, the church as an imperial, territorial force has become overextended. While organic unions, ecumenical coöperation, a World Council are essentially goals, they have been developed at the expense of not mastering the problems of the home base. It is not that these things are not noble achievements; it is that they have no roots, they give a false sense of strength by their external size and structure.

Fourth, the real danger confronting the church is not that it will be destroyed, that it is too weak to perform its function, that it will lack prestige and public respect. The danger is that it will become largely a ceremonial affair, "where people go and sit on comfortable benches, waiting patiently until time to go home to their Sunday dinner." [7] The danger is that religion may become a holy hide-out, a place of retreat into silent pools and eddies of isolation, ignored by the masses and irrelevant.

Fifth, the hope, the real hope we may have, rests in faith upon the essential relevance of the Christian religion. Protestantism is peculiarly equipped, by God's grace, with those things which today requires. Who knows but that she may have a rendezvous with Destiny? [8]

WHAT MUST THE LAYMEN DO?

The idea of the Christian community has special claims on the attention of laymen. This claim grows out of the nature of Protestantism, which is essentially a laymen's movement. It is still true that in America laymen have more to do in determining the nature of the church enterprise than do the clergy.

Under these circumstances all the interest in the church in the community will come to naught unless the lay people become immersed in it. It cannot be a concern of the leaders only.

A layman's platform of faith in the Christian rural community can be built with four planks. The ideal of the Christian community is something to put one's faith into. Laymen should know that believing in the Christian community involves no compromise. To have that hope is to be able to make a declaration of faith. To have it is to experience the expulsive power of a new affection. To have it brings a new experience of Christian brotherhood. To have it gives a man a strong rock on which to stand. It takes a big Christian to have this hope and goal. It gives man a strong faith.

Laymen should consider the doctrine of the church, which holds that the church is the body of Christ and local churches a part of that body. The body of Christ made up of diverse elements held in unity is to be kept whole and intact. It is man's duty and privilege to aid God in this constructive work.

Laymen should keep away from schism, from dividing the church, as they keep away from sin. Not many years ago, a small West Virginia community of about 467 in the village and adjacent area had one Protestant church with a "Union church" background but denominationally related. An active layman, member of another denomination, became disgruntled because he felt he was not recognized. Therefore, he set out to organize a church of his own faith. Now there are two churches in town. One has a membership of 56, an average attendance of 20 at two principal services a month and an average Sunday school attendance of 13. The other church, the parent body, claims 68 members, an average attendance at worship of 50 and at Sunday school 24. Neither church has a resident pastor.

No one will doubt the good intentions of the man who started a new church. Many will applaud his efforts. Others will say, "There is plenty of room for at least two churches, for if all the people attended, the buildings would not hold them." But, alas, the nature of the church is not determined by the number of people a building will hold. The builders of the second and other churches on such narrow margins of population and with such minor ecclesiastical variations may be defeating the will of God. Before taking such steps laymen may well ask, "Is this my will or is it God's will?" The New Testament is against the splitting of churches.

Laymen can in word and deed stand for those things that bring unity and integrity to the rural community. There is a growing number of laymen who use the force of their words and efforts for a united, cooperative Christian community. These ought not to become weary in well doing. Others may well emulate them.

Some laymen are making unique contributions to the growth of the Christian community by giving testimony to their convictions. One man, a cattle dealer, enthusiastic for what the federated church had done to unite his community, became known in several counties as the man who believed in and talked about cows and the federated church wherever he went. He knew both and voiced his convictions. Laymen conversant with all forms of church cooperation and outreach and with tested methods of community service are essential to progress in the movement. The laymen only can make the church a vital force in the community.

References

1. *The Pocket Book of Old Masters*, by Herman J. Wechler, p. 28. New York, Pocket Books Inc., 1949.
2. "A Protestant Program for the Family Farm," p. 58. New York, Committee on Town and Country, 1949.
3. *Town and Country Church*, September, 1947, pp. 5–6.

4. "The Significance of the Community for the Religious Situation," by Maynard L. Cassady, in *Crozer Quarterly*, Vol. XXVI, January, 1949, Number 1, p. 14. Used by permission.

5. *Ibid.*, pp. 16–17. Used by permission.

6. *Ibid.*, pp. 17–18. Used by permission.

7. Quoted line from *Alternative to Futility*, by Elton Trueblood, p. 31. New York, Harper and Brothers, 1948.

8. Cassady, *op. cit.*, p. 18. Used by permission.

CHAPTER 8

Men of Faith

The company of Christian community builders, past and present, encompasses a fellowship of men of great faith. These are men whose names are not generally known to the rank and file of Christians, though they should be. By their comprehension of the Christian mission, their capacity to interpret it and practise it and by their magnanimous spirits, these men are to be numbered among the world's great. Saints of the countryside are Richard Baxter, George Herbert, Charles Kingsley, John Frederic Oberlin, Felix Neff, Harlon S. Mills, Kenyon L. Butterfield, Warren H. Wilson, Mark Dawber, and thousands of others. It is a glorious company, the increase of which will be for the redemption of mankind. Brief pen portraits of three, two from the past and one from the present, will point out the greatness of all.

OBERLIN — PROTESTANT SAINT

The name of John Frederic Oberlin has appeared on the foregoing pages. Since he is probably the most widely known and emulated rural pastor in the world, it is well to review some of his ideas and ideals.

Augustus Field Beard says that Oberlin realized fully that he needed to deal with environment as well as heredity and that it was impossible to save individuals if they were neglected in their community conditions. Oberlin knew his theological certainties, but he knew how to mix his piety with practical utility. A circular that he wrote to his parishioners at Fouday admirably illustrates this balance.

Dear Friends of Fouday, — Several persons at Zolbach have long desired that the road between Fouday and Zolbach, in your district, should be mended and put in good repair. Such a measure would be greatly for the advantage of Fouday. But for whose sake will you do it? Will you do it from love to your heavenly Father? Will you do it from love to the Lord Jesus Christ, who during his stay upon earth went about doing good and who redeemed us to be a peculiar people zealous of good works? Will you do it from love to God's animals which your heavenly Father has created? etc.[1]

Another circular, from his own press, asked these questions among others: "Do you punctually contribute your share towards repairing roads? Have you planted upon the common at least twice as many trees as there are heads in your family? Have you planted them properly, or only as idle and ignorant people would do to save themselves trouble? Have you proper drains in your yards for carrying off the refuse water? Do you keep a dog unless there is absolute necessity?"[2] Oberlin was thus constantly reminding the people of their daily duties as a part of their Christian life.

Always an ardent exponent of his own ideals, he was first to defend others in the same right. A symbolic picture still hangs in Oberlin's study (though he died in 1826). From one point the object portrayed appears to be a bird and from another position a rose. It has been said that Oberlin through this picture illustrated the truth that two honest men could look at the same fact and arrive at different conclusions. At any rate, Oberlin practised great-heartedness and toleration in his mountain villages. He did not want the church to be divided; there were not enough people for that; the gospel was against it. So on a communion Sunday Catholics, Lutherans, and Cal-

vinists received communion at the same time. On the plate
were three kinds of bread; wafers, and leavened and unleavened
bread, so each could partake according to his convictions.

FELIX NEFF — SKY PILOT OF THE ALPS

Another great, but less well known, pastor is Felix Neff,
who lived for a brief span from 1798 to 1829. He also made a
record of parish work that has placed his name in the annals of
distinguished country preachers.

The churches served by Felix Neff were situated in the
province of Dauphiny in France, high in the mountains that
separate France from Italy. Within this area about 18 leagues
in diameter lived nearly 700 Protestants who were associated
with five or six extensive parishes. One writer says that in this
region "Vast and gloomy mountains stretch into the horizon
and hide their hoary summits in the clouds; tottering cliffs
and masses of projecting rocks rise in frowning majesty; whilst
the frozen glacier with its fantastic crest and yawning precipice,
the restless torrent, and the impending avalanche, complete
the outline of the scene."[3]

Not only were the natural conditions such as to make the
pastor's travels most arduous and even dangerous in the winter
season, but living standards among the people were low. Many
of the cottages had no chimneys and were without windows,
and kitchens were dark and noisome hovels seldom cleaned out
more than once a year. "During the seven months of winter,
the whole family are accustomed to reside in the midst of filth
and smoke. Their food and clothes are as coarse and inconveni-
ent as their abodes."[4]

There are a number of characteristics of Felix Neff's ministry
that made him a community-server.

Neff was above controversy. When he went to the mountain
region he found the people steeped in it, but he said, "I will

not lose my time in these discussions so withering to the soul."
Instead, he sought to introduce practical teachings. This attitude gave him the qualities of a builder and a creator of unity.
The energy that might have been wasted in party strife was
instead expended in a monumental ministry to needy communities.

He carried on an arduous ministry over the entire area. On
Sunday he often would travel several leagues and preach as
many as six times, large crowds coming from long distances to
hear him. After having preached from five o'clock in the
morning until seven at night he was happy in his early days to
report that he had no cough or pain in his chest.

Neff adapted his preaching to the natural environment.
He once said, "I have learned all I know from three books: the
Bible, my own heart, and nature. The first of these, through the
grace of God, taught me the other two; and from it also I
learned the perfections and purposes of a holy, just, and merci-
ful God; from the second, I have become acquainted with the
enormity of sin, the wiles of Satan, and the misery, the degradation, and the helplessness of my fallen condition; while from
the book of nature, I draw all my illustrations of the doctrine
I preach."[5]

He taught people to read in order that they might understand the Bible. He supported plans for a Bible society and a
religious tract association.

At the recommendation of the local doctor Neff gathered
and helped prepare plants for the making of medicine to be
used by the mountain people. Interested in a better system of
education, he was responsible for inaugurating projects for the
erection of a school building and for instituting a teacher
training program.

He was well versed in psalmody and taught his people how
to sing. Meetings held on Sundays and during the week often

drew large numbers of people. The evenings were spent in memorizing hymns, tunes as well as words.

Neff led in the construction of a system of irrigation despite the initial opposition of his people.

He introduced improved methods of planting and caring for potatoes. Again the people refused to follow the advice of their pastor until, in his own garden, he had demonstrated an improved method of planting and care that produced crops so much superior to those in the parishioners' fields that they eventually adopted his method.

Deeply disturbed by the poor sanitation and the inferior clothing worn by the people he embarked on a program for their improvement.

He strongly advocated and practised what today is sometimes called the "group method," through which people were trained and "built up" in the Christian life.

Neff had a philosophy of comprehensive Christian work. He regarded the salvation of souls as the chief object of all his exertions and was almost continually occupied in preaching and carrying on other "solemn" duties that belonged to the ministry of the gospel, but yet he found leisure moments to occupy himself with the temporal affairs of the flock. It is said that he gave the lie to the commonly held opinion in the high Alps that none can think seriously of his own salvation or the salvation of others without neglecting temporal obligations. "The rapid progress of improvement and amelioration, which now took place, furnishes an illustration of the fact that no sooner do the truths of the gospel obtain their legitimate power over the soul, than they begin to exercise that benign and humanizing influence which renders them the most efficient means of civilization."[6] Neff set a high standard for any church seeking to serve its community, in spite of primitive conditions and the lack of community agencies.

MARK A. DAWBER —
VERSATILE PROPHET OF TODAY

"The dynamo of human life is community; without it life would run down. . . . Community is something more than a place, it is a state of mind and a spiritual fellowship; hence of all institutions the Christian church should have for it a special concern. . . . Christianity is a religion of relationships; we must save the community if we are to save the individual; we urgently need a theology of community redemption. . . . Most of our Protestant churches are not community institutions; often the church is the most divisive factor. . . . Making the community Christian is not going to happen as a result of a few preachments from the pulpit; it is an educational task that must penetrate all the agencies and activities of the community."

Who is this prophet whose voice has at once a modern and a first-century ring? He finds encouragement in signs of a developing American interest in community, but he sees grave danger in mass exploitation of the individual by the forces of secularism and self-interest. Particularly does he fear the secularizing effect on rural life of such developments as mechanization of agriculture, industrialization of rural occupations, centralization of educational and social services, transportation and communication. Not evil in themselves, these are trends, he says, that cannot be stemmed by the church and must not be ignored. They offer a challenge for the rechurching of America.

Mark A. Dawber grew up in England in the Cheshire village of Knutsford. Here he experienced a kind of community pattern that seems to him now a practical device for putting his gospel to work in America. Its secret is the Church of England concept of the parish as a geographical unit inclusive of all the people living within its boundaries. Life in Knutsford centered about the church. Dissenters attended chapel on Sunday afternoons, but they remained integral parts of the parish and shared in its activities. Education, recreation, social life, everything pertaining to community well-being became parish business.

This seemed to Mark Dawber natural and right. It came to him as something of a shock when as a young couple he and his wife visited relatives in Pennsylvania to find that the pattern had not carried over across the water.

In Dallas, suburb of Wilkes-Barre, he found the organ in the Wesleyan Church out of repair. As a student at the London College of Music he had specialized in church music and especially the organ. Soon he had the Dallas organ in working order, and the congregation invited him to stay on and play for their services. Then he began preaching, and it was not long before he and Mrs. Dawber found themselves established in the Maple Grove four-point rural parish in Pennsylvania's Wyoming Valley. This meant four services every Sunday and ministry to families in a two hundred square mile area.

Here was a chance to give the parish philosophy a trial, to cultivate in the valley among the people of four churches a sense of interest in one another, a feeling of shared experience and interdependence. One evening every week became a meeting time for everybody in the parish, sometimes in one church, sometimes in another. Beginning with simple group recreation, the gatherings increased in popularity. Choral societies and discussion groups on a variety of subjects of common interest drew general participation. Life took on new color and significance as people learned to know their neighbors and to comprehend the community of interest underlying the lives of all of them.

After four years in the Wyoming Valley, in 1918 Mark Dawber was called by Boston University to become Professor of Rural Church. In the academic world he found other thinkers whose ideas coincided with his. There was Dr. Kenyon L.

Butterfield, President of the Massachusetts College of Agriculture. A member of the Roosevelt Country Life Commission, Dr. Butterfield felt a deep concern for the rural community parish. At Hartford Theological Seminary and Yale Divinity School, Dr. Malcolm Dana was making popular the larger-parish concept. Meantime Dr. Warren H. Wilson of the Presbyterian Board of National Missions was busily setting up demonstration parishes and inspiring larger service through cooperation.

Basic to this philosophy of the church-centered community is the conviction that the preservation and transmission of the gains of civilization can be accomplished only through wholesome community life, that democracy and Christianity alike achieve significant development only as they find expression in the immediate personal relationships of people.

Going from Boston University to the Department of Rural Work of the Methodist Board of Missions and Church Extension, Dr. Dawber continued to preach and practise his doctrine far and wide. At the colleges of agriculture at Cornell and the University of Wisconsin his name became a household word. Pastors of all denominations felt as free to seek his counsel as did the ministers of his own communion. He had a large part in organizing the first larger parish in Tompkins County, New York, and he gave encouragement and counsel to numerous small churches seeking the way to effective service through cooperation. Concerned that the church take the offensive as witness in the drive for community, he gave an energetic boost to local interchurch cooperation.

When in 1938 the Home Missions Council of North America sought a new executive, the choice fell naturally upon Dr. Dawber. This new position enlarged the scope of his activities, gave him a nation-wide and church-wide laboratory in which to put his ideas to work. Constituent to the council are the home mission boards of the leading Protestant communions; today they number twenty-three. Further, Puerto Rico, Alaska, Hawaii, the Virgin Islands, and the Canal Zone are included in home mission territory, and these outposts are feeling the influence of the Dawber message.

On government dam sites, where populations of several thousand appear overnight and stay indefinitely in new housing projects; in growing cities, new churches become an urgent need. What kind shall they be? The Home Missions Council has an answer, growing out of the conviction that the church should build the community.

When an influx of workers and their families moved into southern Nevada to construct what is now Hoover Dam, there was no church at all. Home missions boards of seven denominations pooled resources to send in a minister and establish a church. As the dam neared completion, maintenance staff came in to stay and Boulder City became a thriving settled community. Within nine years Grace Community Church had ceased to require national mission support, and today it makes its own annual contribution to the work of its parent body, the Home Missions Council.

Under Dr. Dawber's leadership, the work of the Home Missions Council among Negro sharecroppers and tenant farmers in the South extends the community philosophy. Through institutes and extension classes, it aims to educate rural Negro ministers in the concept of the church-centered community with the pastor as leader. Homemade low-cost housing, church construction, improved agricultural methods all become as integral a part of the pastoral job as Sunday preaching. Beginning with one extension worker in one area in Georgia, this program now functions in ten Southern states. In addition to the training of ministers, it provides courses for church women leaders, and in Arkansas, extensive work with teen-age boys and girls. Generous grants from the General Education Board of the Rockefeller Foundation and the Phelps-Stokes Fund have helped materially in the development of this program and have made possible the establishment of rural church departments in eleven Negro theological seminaries.

To Dr. Dawber, the local community is the proving ground for all that we would undertake in our national life. It is here that the individual assumes his true stature, a stature that he possesses nowhere else. Here he can be at home, have personal security and recognition, give expression to his concerns, assume responsibility for the atmosphere in which his children shall grow up.

Thoreau at Walden casts no spell on this community-minded man. He does not see how a man can tackle the job of Christian life by himself. Man has no chance to win if he works alone. But the accidental quality of his own individual success or failure becomes negligible when as part of a fellowship he aims at this realistic idea of a Christian community.

Organized evil calls for organized righteousness, he reiterates. From experience he knows that organizing the top forces of righteousness on the interdenominational level is hard going, but that it is an easy business compared to translating principles and policies into workable techniques in small communities. Yet that is where the job must be done.

Dr. Dawber has shocked many an audience with the pronouncement: "The trouble with the church is *too many ministers*." What he means, of course, is that there are too many ministers untrained in techniques of education and community leadership, that the pastoral job today calls for specialists skilled in penetrating educational and social activities with Christian philosophy. For a rural parish staff he suggests a minimum of three persons: a minister responsible for preaching and administration, a religious education director to lead an educational and social program for all age groups; and a pastor and personal counselor. Just as the rural school has found it necessary to consolidate and move to a more logical center of operation, so must the church consider the geographical and denominational readjustments necessary to provide adequate resources to meet the needs.

Looking toward his retirement from the Home Missions Council following the national Home Missions Congress in January, 1950, Dr. Dawber early in 1949 accepted appointment as pastor of the People's Church in Long Beach, Long Island. As years before in Dallas, Pennsylvania, he had endeared himself at the outset by his artistic skill, so he did at Long Beach, this time not as organist but as wood carver. He learned that his congregation had ordered a new altar from a commercial firm and were planning an Easter dedication service. A few weeks before Easter, the disturbing news came that circumstances beyond control would delay delivery of the altar for several months.

The son of John Dawber, cabinetmaker of Knutsford, England, was determined that his people should not be disappointed. He had done no carving for forty-five years, but he still had his carving tools, all sixty of them. He managed to get somewhere in New York a piece of Italian limewood; he set up a bench in his garage and went to work. He was still serving the Home Missions Council as well as the Long Beach Church, and his office staff wondered why during the days before Easter the three o'clock train developed such an attraction for their intrepid head, who had always been the last to leave at night. On Maundy Thursday the secret came out, when at an interdenominational service in the Congregational Christian chapel on Fourth Avenue in New York there was displayed an eloquent carved replica of Leonardo de Vinci's "Last Supper." Working from early dinner till past midnight, Dr. Dawber had completed his labor of love in seven days. On Easter Sunday the "Last Supper" was installed in the altar of the People's Church at Long Beach at a memorable dedication service.

A suburban commuting town and summer resort on the south shore of Long Island, Long Beach is dominantly Jewish and Roman Catholic, yet it has four Protestant churches. Many of its 15,000 winter residents rent their homes and go elsewhere for the summer season, when the population soars to 70,000. Not an easy setting in which to instill a sense of community! Dr. Dawber found his People's Church well organized in terms of activities, with many Jewish and Roman Catholic families participating in the social program. Under his stimulus the congregation is mapping out the parish territory with a breakdown into sections for which various members take responsibility for keeping in touch with residents, whether or not they are affiliated with the People's Church. The manse, a tidy, brown-shingled bungalow on Reynolds Bay, could be either a refuge for a retired scholar or a house-by-the-side-of-the-road. Already there is no question as to which it shall be.

No one has a more sensitive and realistic appreciation of Dr. Dawber as man and servant of Christ than his friend Hermann N. Morse, past president of the Home Missions Council and general secretary of the Board of National Missions of the Presbyterian Church in the U. S. A. Dr. Morse says of him:

His whole career has been characterized by courage, by vision and imagination, and by a prodigious, tireless energy. He has exemplified, as fully and genuinely as anyone I know, the Master's concern, which is the missionary concern, for the poor, the handicapped, all who have been hardly dealt with by circumstances. He has eloquently pleaded their cause; he has had a rare gift of irritating the right people on their behalf; better still, he has been constantly initiating constructive programs for their benefit. He has been no mere champion of lost causes, thank God, but he has helped the church and many agencies outside the church to see and accept their obligation of service and sharing. He has made a unique place for himself in the life and work of the church.

To have such a leader in American Protestantism is heartening; to have such dynamic ideals back of the policy-making in American home missions is a reason for hope.

FORWARD THEN

The desire for a Christian community is set deeply in the human heart. People want a wholesome community that provides the basic satisfactions for living; they want a church that unites the community. Of course, many want the individual church, the denomination, the sect to be first and last.

But men at their best want unity within, unity with neighbors, unity in the community. Let them falter and fail, make mistakes in attitude, conception, organization, and techniques; yet men long for the kind of church that brings this unity and strength.

So then, let all press forward toward the ideal in order:

That the spirit of unity that was in Christ be injected into the bloodstream of the church;

That the gospel of unity be not watered down but that it be a concentration of the vital elements of the gospel;

That the church practising unity may be electrified until the hearts of people are warmed to express their love with power, unity, and strength;

That the gospel be received for all of life, a union of altar and home, of preaching and practice, of worship and work;

That the church serving the community may be the instrument for incorporating into its very structure the kind of life that was in Christ.

There is a lively hope that the rural church community can become a place for greatness, greatness in the ministry and greatness among the laity, greatness in the individual and greatness in the corporate structure. England has set an example in the English country parsonage, which through its incumbents and their children and through laymen has given to the nation some of its greatest leaders. The ideals and practices of the whole English speaking world have been raised by the lofty literature that had its source in the country parish.

The ultimate hope for rural people is that they become what they can become when Christ is central in their lives. For this to happen the influences of Christ must permeate all facets of community life. Throughout history there have been two distinct and contrasting trends: the one toward pietism or withdrawal from the normal, active life of the community; the other toward a projecting of the Christian faith into the life of the community or people. The interest in the community belongs in this latter trend. The redemption of men depends upon it.

The community permeated with the thinking, spirit, and love of Christ will be an added force in bringing people into fullness of life in him. The Christian community helps men to sense anew fellowship with Christ who loved the country things and country people, the Christ who makes men new in him.

References

1. From *The Story of John Frederic Oberlin*, by Augustus Field Beard. Boston, The Pilgrim Press, 1909. Used by permission.
2. *Ibid.* Used by permission.
3. *Life of Felix Neff*, pp. 68, 69. London, The Religious Tract Society, 1836.
4. *Ibid.*, p. 88.
5. *Ibid.*, p. 62.
6. *Ibid.*, p. 126.

BIBLIOGRAPHY

RURAL LIFE

American Farmer, The, by Lee Fryer. New York, Harper and Brothers, 1947. $3.00.

Farmer and the Rest of Us, The, by Arthur Moore. Boston, Little, Brown and Company, 1945. $2.50.

Our Plundered Planet, by Fairfield Osborn. Boston, Little, Brown and Company, 1948. $2.50.

Rural America Today: Its School and Community Life, by George A. Works and Simon O. Lesser. Chicago, University of Chicago Press, 1942. $3.75.

Rural Community Organization, by Dwight Sanderson and Robert A. Polson. New York, John Wiley and Sons, Inc., 1939. $3.00.

Sociology of Rural Life, The, by T. Lynn Smith. New York, Harper and Brothers, 1940. $3.75.

Study of Rural Society, A, by J. H. Kolb and Edmund de S. Brunner. Boston, Houghton Mifflin Company, 1946 (third edition). $4.50.

THE RURAL COMMUNITY

Locating the Rural Community, by Dwight Sanderson. Extension Bulletin, No. 413, College of Agriculture, Cornell University, Ithaca, New York, 1939. 5 cents.

Measuring the Effectiveness of Your Community, by Douglass Ensminger. Extension Bulletin No. 444, College of Agriculture, Cornell University, Ithaca, New York, 1940.

Rural Community, The, by Dwight Sanderson. Boston, Ginn and Company, 1932. $4.40.

Small Community, The, by Arthur E. Morgan. New York, Harper and Brothers, 1942. $3.00 cloth; $1.50 paper.

Small Community Looks Ahead, The, by Wayland J. Hayes. New York, Harcourt Brace and Company, 1947. $3.00.

Your Community: Its Provision for Health, Education, Safety, and Welfare, by Joanna C. Colcord. New York, Russell Sage Foundation, 1947. $1.50.

THE RURAL CHURCH

Christian Enterprise Among Rural People, The. New York, Rural Missions Cooperating Committee of the Foreign Missions Conference of North America, 1945. $1.50.

Church in Our Town, The, by Rockwell C. Smith. New York, Abingdon-Cokesbury Press, 1945. $1.50.

Church in the Rural Community, The, by William C. Martin. Board of Education and Church Extension, The Methodist Church, 150 Fifth Avenue, New York 11, 1948. 50 cents.

Gospel in Action, The, by Henry W. McLaughlin. Richmond, John Knox Press, 1944. $1.00.

Manifesto on Rural Life. National Catholic Rural Life Conference; Milwaukee, The Bruce Publishing Company, 1939. $1.50 cloth; $1.00 paper.

Manual for Town and Country Churches, A, by Henry S. Randolph. New York, Board of National Missions of the Presbyterian Church in the U. S. A., 1947. $1.00.

Rural Life and the Church, by David E. Lindstrom. Champaign, Illinois, The Garrard Press, 1946. $2.50.

Story of John Frederic Oberlin, The, by Augustus Field Beard. The Christian Rural Fellowship, 156 Fifth Avenue, New York 10, 1946 (reprint of an earlier book published by Pilgrim Press). 25 cents.

THE CHURCH IN THE COMMUNITY

Characteristics of a Christian Rural Community, The, by Stanley E. Skinner. Christian Rural Fellowship Bulletin No. 59, 156 Fifth Avenue, New York 10, 1941. 5 cents.

Characteristics of a Christian Rural Community, The, by Eugene Smathers. Christian Rural Fellowship Bulletin No. 61, 156 Fifth Avenue, New York 10, 1941. 5 cents.

Rural Church Program that Makes Religion the Qualifying Factor in Every Experience of Life, A, by Eugene Smathers. Christian Rural Fellowship Bulletin No. 66, 156 Fifth Avenue, New York 10, 1941. 5 cents.

CHURCH COOPERATION

Art of Church Cooperation, The, by Ralph A. Felton. Madison, New Jersey, Felton. 25 cents.

Cooperative Churches, by Ralph A. Felton. Madison, New Jersey, Felton. 20 cents.

Group Ministry Plan, The, by Aaron H. Rapking. Board of Education and Church Extension, The Methodist Church, 150 Fifth Avenue, New York 11. Free.

Grouping, by Ward W. Hibbs. Parkersburg, West Virginia, Baptist State Convention. 5 cents.

Larger Parish: An Effective Organization for Rural Churches, The, by Mark Rich. Extension Bulletin No. 408, College of Agriculture, Cornell University, Ithaca, New York, 1939. 5 cents.

Life in the Larger Parish, by Margaret J. Harris. Committee on Town and Country, 297 Fourth Avenue, New York 10, 1944. 25 cents.

Manual for a Local Council of Church Women or a Woman's Department of a Council of Churches. The United Council of Church Women, 156 Fifth Avenue, New York 10. 20 cents.

One Foot on the Land, by Ralph A. Felton. Madison, New Jersey, Felton. 30 cents.

Pastoral Unity Plan, The, by Edwin L. Becker. Indianapolis, The United Christian Missionary Society, 1946. 25 cents.

Size of a Rural Parish, The, by Ralph A. Felton. Madison, New Jersey, Felton. 5 cents.

WORSHIP

Hymns of the Rural Spirit. Federal Council of the Churches of Christ in America, 297 Fourth Avenue, New York 10, 1947. 35 cents a copy postpaid; rates on quantities.

Prayers for Rural Life. New York, Department of Domestic Missions of the Protestant Episcopal Church. 5 cents.

Rural Life Prayers, compiled by Mark Rich. Commission on Worship, 297 Fourth Avenue, New York 10, 1950.

Note: Orders of worship are prepared each year for the observance of Rural Life Sunday and Harvest Festival. These are available from the Committee on Town and Country, 297 Fourth Avenue, New York 10. Single copies 5 cents; rates on quantities.

MISCELLANEOUS

Church at Work in the Rural Community, by V. A. Edwards. Nashville, Sunday School Publication Board, The National Baptist Convention, U. S. A., Inc. 50 cents.

Church in Cooperation with Community Agencies, The. Chicago, International Council of Religious Education, 1936.

How the Church Grows, by Roy A. Burkhart. New York, Harper and Brothers, 1947. $2.00.

Protestant Program for the Family Farm, A. Committee on Town and Country, 297 Fourth Avenue, New York 10, 1949. 35 cents.

Rural Communities in Wisconsin. Circular No. 353, Extension Service, University of Wisconsin, Madison, 1945.

School Centralization and the Rural Community, by Dwight Sanderson. Extension Bulletin No. 455, College of Agriculture, Cornell University, Ithaca, New York, 1941. 5 cents.

PERIODICALS

Christian Rural Fellowship Bulletin. The Christian Rural Fellowship, 156 Fifth Avenue, New York 10. Ten issues annually; $1.00.

Community Service News. Community Service, Inc., Yellow Springs, Ohio. Bimonthly; $1.25.

Rural Sociology. The Rural Sociological Society, North Carolina State College of Agriculture and Engineering, University of North Carolina, Raleigh. Quarterly; $3.50.

Town and Country Church. Committee on Town and Country, 297 Fourth Avenue, New York. Nine issues annually; $1.00.

INDEX